Official Publisher Partnership

OCR
TEXT PROCESSING
(BUSINESS PROFESSIONAL)
LEVEL 3 BOOK **1**

TEXT PRODUCTION, WORD PROCESSING
AND AUDIO TRANSCRIPTION

EDITOR: JILL DOWSON

ROSALIND BUXTON • LESLEY DAKIN • SYLVIA ELKINS • SUE FOX
• BEVERLY LORAM • JEAN RAY • PAM SMITH • SARAH WAREING

HODDER
EDUCATION
AN HACHETTE UK COMPANY

Orders: please contact Bookpoint Ltd, 130 Milton Park, Abingdon, Oxon OX14 4SB.
Telephone: +44 (0)1235 827720. Fax: +44 (0)1235 400454. Lines are open from 9.00am to 5.00pm,
Monday to Saturday, with a 24-hour message-answering service. You can also order through our website
www.hoddereducation.co.uk

If you have any comments to make about this, or any of our other titles, please send them to
educationenquiries@hodder.co.uk

British Library Cataloguing in Publication Data
A catalogue record for this title is available from the British Library

ISBN: 978 1 444 10790 6

First Edition Published 2010
Impression number   10 9 8 7 6 5 4 3 2 1
Year   2013 2012 2011 2010

Hachette UK's policy is to use papers that are natural, renewable and
recyclable products and made from wood grown in sustainable forests.
The logging and manufacturing processes are expected to conform to the
environmental regulations of the country of origin.

Cover photo © Influx Productions/Getty Images
Typeset by Dorchester Typesetting Group Ltd
Printed in Malta for Hodder Education, an Hachette UK company, 338 Euston Road, London NW1 3BH

CONTENTS

Worked Examples

Worked examples for all exercises and exams are available to download in PDF format on the Hodder Plus website: www.hodderplus.co.uk/ocrtextprocessing.

THE AUTHORS

The following authors, who have provided all the material for this book, are Chief Examiners/Examiners for the Oxford, Cambridge and RSA Examination Board: Rosalind Buxton, Lesley Dakin, Sylvia Elkins, Sue Fox, Beverly Loram, Jean Ray, Pam Smith and Sarah Wareing. The Series Editor is Jill Dowson.

STUDENT TEXTBOOKS IN THE TEXT PROCESSING (BUSINESS PROFESSIONAL) SUITE PUBLISHED BY HODDER EDUCATION, ENDORSED BY OCR EXAMINATIONS BOARD

Level 1 – Book 1 Text Production – core unit Word Processing Audio-Transcription	Level 1 – Book 2 Mailmerge Business Presentations Legal Text Processing
Level 2 – Book 1* Text Production – core unit Word Processing Audio-Transcription	Level 2 – Book 2 Medical Word Processing Medical Audio-Transcription Legal Audio-Transcription
Level 2 – Book 3 Mailmerge Business Presentations Document Presentation	
Level 3 – Book 1 Text Production – core unit Word Processing Audio-Transcription	Level 3 – Book 2 Legal Word Processing Document Presentation

* Level 2 – Book 1 is available to order from the Hodder Education website (www.hoddereducation.co.uk). Level 1 – Book 1 and Level 3 – Book 1 will be published early in 2010. Material covering the other units is also planned for 2010.

INTRODUCTION

About the book

This series of textbooks is designed for you to build on the knowledge and skills you have already acquired so that you can progress to more advanced and varied text processing work in order to gain an Award, Certificate and Diploma in Text Processing (Business Professional).

It presumes that you already have a knowledge of the keyboard and how to use Microsoft® Word to produce business documents.

This book contains the background information, practice exercises and practice exams you require to prepare for the OCR Text Processing (Business Professional) exam units in:

- Text Production Level 3
- Word Processing Level 3
- Audio-Transcription Level 3.

The book is divided into the following sections.

- **Introduction:** this covers the contents of the book, together with an overview of the Text Processing (Business Professional) suite of qualifications at Level 3.
- **Assessment Criteria:** this section contains the syllabuses, or unit contents, at the time of going to press for the three units. Each syllabus lists the items you will be tested on in the exams, and the relevant knowledge, understanding and skills that you need to acquire in order to complete these exams. It also gives details of the marking schemes, complete with tutors' notes, so that you can see exactly how your exam paper will be marked. Visit the Text Processing pages of the OCR website for any unit updates.
- **Knowledge, Understanding and Skills:** this section provides detailed notes together with exercises that enable you to practise the skills you need to master before attempting a full practice exam for each unit. Following each set of notes, there are three examples of each type of document. Templates and recall text are available on the Hodder Plus website at **www.hodderplus.co.uk/ocrtextprocessing**.
- **Exam work:** this section provides hints for exam work, together with three new practice exams similar to the OCR standard for each unit. Templates and recall text are available on the Hodder Plus website at **www.hodderplus.co.uk/ocrtextprocessing**.

- **Worked examples:** correct worked examples of all practice exercises and exams are supplied in this section, which is available to download in PDF format on the Hodder Plus website. Note that each of these shows only one way of displaying the documents – for example, your method of emphasis may not be the same, your line ends may differ slightly or you may have left extra linespacing after headings. This is acceptable, as long as you have followed instructions and formatted your document consistently.

The Text Processing (Business Professional) suite of qualifications

Overview of Level 3

The Text Processing suite of qualifications has been designed to develop and recognise candidates' ability to produce a variety of current and straightforward business documents to meet the requirements of the employer in a modern business environment. The units that make up these qualifications have been developed from the RSA Text Processing Modular Awards Stage III, which have been widely recognised by employers as benchmark qualifications in text processing. The qualifications are nationally accredited on to the Qualifications & Credit Framework (QCF).

The qualifications at Level 3 are suitable for candidates who:

- have sufficient skill, underpinning knowledge and command of English to carry out the production of complex business documents without supervision
- are following programmes of study in administration at Level 3
- are already employed in text processing or administrative-related job roles, and wish to further develop their knowledge and expertise in this area in preparation for employment in senior job roles.

Qualification structures

Candidates enter each unit separately and a unit certificate will be issued. On achievement of each unit the candidate will be awarded a number of credits. If a candidate wishes to achieve a Text Processing (Business Professional) Award, Certificate or Diploma, credits will need to be accumulated as described in the boxes on pages 4 and 5.

OCR Text Processing (Business Professional) Level 3 Award – 06961 (English)/04609 (Welsh)

The full OCR Level 3 Award in Text Processing (Business Professional) is awarded when the candidate has successfully completed **units to the value of at least 11 credits**.

- Six of these credits must come from a Level 3 core unit: Text Production, Cynhyrchu Testun (Welsh) or Text Production – Screen Reader. The assessment criteria is almost identical for each version of the core unit, therefore candidates may choose only one.
- The remaining five credits can be taken from the Level 3 optional units listed in OCR's Centre Handbook.
- In order to receive the Welsh Award (Dyfarniad Lefel 3), a candidate should be entered for the core unit (03949) and 04606 as their optional unit.

Please note that some combinations of units are barred – for full details of rules of combination candidates should refer to their centres or access the OCR website on www.ocr.org.uk

OCR Text Processing (Business Professional) Level 3 Certificate – 06962

The full OCR Level 3 Certificate in Text Processing (Business Professional) is awarded when the candidate has successfully completed **units to the value of at least 20 credits**.

- Six of these credits must come from a Level 3 core unit: Text Production, Cynhyrchu Testun (Welsh) or Text Production – Screen Reader. The assessment criteria is almost identical for each version of the core unit, therefore candidates may choose only one.
- Of the remaining credits, a minimum of six must be taken from the Level 3 optional units listed in OCR's Centre Handbook.
- Further credits required may be taken from Entry Level Speed Keying.

Please note that some combinations of units are barred – for full details of rules of combination candidates should refer to their centres or access the OCR website on www.ocr.org.uk

OCR Text Processing (Business Professional) Level 3 Diploma – 06963
The full OCR Level 3 Diploma in Text Processing (Business Professional) is awarded when the candidate has successfully completed **units to the value of at least 37 credits**.

- Six of these credits must come from a Level 3 core unit: Text Production, Cynhyrchu Testun (Welsh) or Text Production – Screen Reader. The assessment criteria is almost identical for each version of the core unit, therefore candidates may choose only one.
- Of the remaining credits, a minimum of 17 must be taken from the Level 3 optional units listed in OCR's Centre Handbook.
- Further credits required may be taken from Entry Level Speed Keying.

Please note that some combinations of units are barred – for full details of rules of combination candidates should refer to their centres or access the OCR website on www.ocr.org.uk

The credits attached to the units achieved within each qualification are banked and may then contribute to the next qualification at the same level (eg if a candidate has achieved the required credit for the Level 3 Award, this credit can also be carried forward to the Level 3 Certificate).

Due to the flexible nature of qualifications within the QCF, these banked credits may also contribute to a higher qualification at a later stage of the candidate's progress.

Form of assessment

Each unit within these qualifications is assessed via an OCR-set and marked examination.

Candidates will be required to carry out all assessment tasks within a stated error tolerance.

Results will be graded Distinction, Pass or Fail, depending upon the number of faults incurred, with the exception of the Shorthand Speed Skills and Speed Keying units, which will state the words per minute speed achieved on the certificate.

Units

Details of the unit contents for Text Processing, Word Processing and Audio-Transcription at Level 3 are provided in this book.

The flexibility of qualifications within the Qualifications & Credit Framework means that candidates may take units at a higher or lower level than the level of their full qualification. The percentages allowed are described in the rules of combination contained within the table for each qualification.

Group 1: core units

03932	Text Production	6 credits
03949	Cynhyrchu Testun	6 credits
00007	Text Production Screen Reader	6 credits

Group 2: optional units

Level 3 Text Processing units

03933	Audio-Transcription	5 credits
03934	Document Presentation	6 credits
03935	Legal Word Processing	6 credits
03936	Shorthand Speed Skills	6 credits
03937	Speed Keying	5 credits
03938	Word Processing	6 credits
04606	Prosesu Geiriau	6 credits

Level 3 iTQ units (Scheme 06611, Test and Trial Units only)

A/500/7290	Email	6 credits
M/500/6783	Word Processing Software	8 credits

Group 3: optional units

Level 2 Text Processing units

06976	Audio-Transcription	4 credits
06977	Business Presentations	5 credits
06978	Document Presentation	5 credits
06980	Legal Audio-Transcription	5 credits
06994	Mailmerge	5 credits
06995	Medical Audio-Transcription	5 credits
06996	Medical Word Processing	5 credits
06997	Shorthand Speed Skills	5 credits
06998	Speed Keying	4 credits
06999	Word Processing	5 credits
03948	Prosesu Geiriau	5 credits

Level 2 iTQ units (Scheme 06611, Test and Trials Units only)

F/500/7288	Email	4 credits
M/500/7304	Presentation Software	6 credits
H/500/6781	Word Processing Software	6 credits

Level 1 Text Processing units

06967	Audio-Transcription	4 credits
06968	Business Presentations	4 credits
06969	Computer Keyboard Skills	3 credits
06970	Legal Text Processing	4 credits
06971	Mailmerge	4 credits
06972	Shorthand Speed Skills	4 credits
06973	Speed Keying	4 credits
06974	Word Processing	4 credits
03946	Prosesu Geiriau	4 credits

Level 1 iTQ units (Scheme 06611 Test and Trial units only)

T/500/7286	Email	2 credits
K/500/7303	Presentation Software	4 credits
J/500/7292	Word Processing Software	4 credits

Entry Level Text Processing unit

06965	Speed Keying	2 credits

At the time of printing, the new QCF iTQ units cannot be used for Text Processing (Business Professional) qualifications.

ASSESSMENT CRITERIA

Unit contents

The following syllabuses give details of the unit contents for Text Production, Word Processing and Audio-Transcription at Level 3. They are updated from time to time by OCR and the current versions are available on the OCR website at **www.ocr.org.uk**.

The first section of each syllabus covers the following aspects:

- **Learning outcomes:** listed in the first column of the table, these describe the tasks that you will be able to carry out once you have acquired the necessary skills to complete the exam at this level.
- **Assessment criteria:** described in the second column of the table, they show the way in which your skills will be assessed in the exam.
- **Knowledge, understanding and skills:** detailed in the third column of the table, they describe the information you need to enable you to complete the exam.

The second section of each document covers the following:

- Unit aim
- Assessment
- Administration guidance
- Guidance on assessment and evidence requirements.

The third section of each document covers the following:

- **Marking criteria:** described in the first column of the table, they show the ways in which your work will be assessed.
- **Tutor notes:** listed in the second column of the table, these give further details about how an exam is marked. Although drafted for tutors, this information will give you invaluable help when you are working towards the exam.

TEXT PROCESSING (BUSINESS PROFESSIONAL)

Text Production
03932

Level: 3

Credits: 6

Learning Time: 60 hours

Learning outcomes	Assessment criteria	Knowledge, understanding and skills
1 Use a word processor or a typewriter efficiently	1.1 Use the different functions of a word processor or different parts of a typewriter	• Set left, right, top and bottom margins of at least 13 mm • Alter linespacing (single/double) as instructed • Emphasise text as instructed
2 Enter and format text from handwritten and typewritten drafts	2.1 Produce text accurately and efficiently from manuscript and from typescript drafts	• Plan and organise work within deadlines • Read and transcribe variable quality manuscript • Plan layout of work in a variety of formats • Accurately key in text from handwritten and typewritten drafts • Interpret written instructions • Check accuracy of amendments and that all instructions have been carried out correctly • Proofread and correct errors, using appropriate correction techniques, to ensure work is 100% accurate • Use consistent style and format of presentation with at least one clear linespace before and after separate items within a document

		• Use appropriate stationery • Use English and mother-tongue dictionaries
3 Produce three business documents	3.1 Key in and print a business letter on pre-printed letterhead or by use of a template from handwritten draft	• Use conventional and consistent layout and style of a business letter • Insert today's date on letter • Use post-dating as instructed • Use OCR supplied letterhead template • *Our ref* and *Your ref* details are keyed in as shown in draft, including capitalisation • Insert a special mark, as indicated on the draft • Insert a subject heading, as indicated on the draft • Indicate enclosures if required, as implied in the draft, using an acceptable convention
	3.2 Key in and print one of the following documents from a handwritten draft: – fax – minutes – terms of reference/ contract	• Use conventional and consistent layout and style of a variety of business documents • Rearrange numbered items as implied **Fax:** • must be produced on OCR fax template • Insert today's date against date heading • Use 2-4 columns to display a list **Minutes:** • Insert an 'Action' column if requested • Use 2-4 columns to display a list

		Terms of Reference/ Contract: • Use 2-4 columns to display a list, eg project team list
	3.3 Key in and print an article or report from handwritten and typewritten draft	• Use conventional and consistent layout and style of a report or article • Insert a page number on continuation sheets • Use single/double linespacing as instructed • Emphasise text, as instructed • Underline text, as shown in the draft • Inset text from left margin • Insert footnotes on the same page as the original footnote indication • Centre text as instructed
	3.4 Amend text as instructed	Amend text as shown in draft: • deletion with replacement words • deletion without replacement words • follow correction signs:

new paragraph   ⌐   or   //

run on

insertion with word(s) above ⋋ or balloon with arrow eg

transpose horizontally ⌒ or balloon with arrow eg

transpose vertically

close up

leave a space

stet _ _ _ _ _ _ with ✓ in margin

no marginal instructions

	3.5 Expand abbreviations, ensuring correct spellings	• Expand abbreviations shown in the list below:

a/c(s)	account(s)	mtg(s)	meeting(s)
appt(s)	appointment(s)	misc	miscellaneous
approx	approximate(ly)	necy	necessary
asap	as soon as possible	opp(s)	opportunity(ies)
cat(s)	catalogue(s)	org(s)	organisation(s)
co(s)	company(ies)	poss	possible

	conf(s)	conference(s)	ref(d)	refer(red)
	dr	dear	ref(s)	reference(s)
	dept(s)	department(s)	sec(s)	secretary(ies)
	doc(s)	document(s)	sig(s)	signature(s)
	emp	employment	temp	temporary
	gntee(s)	guarantee(s)	tel	telephone
	immed	immediate(ly)	yr(s)	year(s)
	info	information	yr(s)	your(s)
	mfr(s)	manufacturer(s)		

days of the week (eg Thur, Fri)
months of the year (eg Jan, Feb)
words in addresses (eg Rd, St, Ave, Dr, Sq, Cres, Pl, Pk)
complimentary close (eg ffly, sncly)

	3.6 Check and correct material containing typographical errors, errors of agreement, punctuation, spelling errors	Identify and correct errors in the draft, including:
		• typographical errors including words containing extra, omitted and transposed letters and extraneous symbols
		• errors of agreement including those of subject/verb and quantity/noun
		• punctuation errors including omitted full stop and omitted initial capital at the start of a sentence
		• apostrophe errors including misplaced and superfluous apostrophes
		• spelling errors in words given below including their derivations where marked * eg plurals, prefixes (such as un-, in- dis-, ir-), suffixes (such as -ed, -ing, -ment, -tion, -ly, -able, -ible, -ence, -ial):

access*	expense*
accommodate*	experience*
achieve*	finance*
acknowledge*	foreign
advertise*	govern*
although	convenient*
apparent*	permanent*
appreciate*	receipt*
believe*	receive*
business*	recommend*
cancel*	responsible*
client*	satisfactory*
colleague*	separate*
committee*	success*
correspond*	sufficient*

		definite* develop* discuss* employ*	support* temporary* through fortunate*
	3.7 Insert a table within text	• Key in a table from handwritten draft, which will not include ruling but candidates may insert lines of ruling if desired • Key in 2-4 columns of data containing text • Key in column headings as shown in the draft • Ensure text in columns and column headings are aligned consistently	
	3.8 Locate information from a resource sheet to include in a document	• Select and insert additional information (such as a name or job title) that will be found in a resource sheet	

Unit aim

This unit aims to equip candidates with the ability to produce, from handwritten and typewritten draft material, a variety of routine business documents to a standard that meets the business document production requirements of employment.

Assessment

Assessment will consist of producing three business documents totalling 1100 words and will take the form of a 1 hour 15 minute test set and marked by OCR.

Results will be graded Distinction, Pass or Fail.

To achieve a Distinction, candidates must produce the documents with no more than 6 faults within the time allowed (1 hour 15 minutes).

To achieve a Pass, candidates must produce the documents with no more than 17 faults within the time allowed (1 hour 15 minutes).

The grade achieved will be stated on the certificate.

Administration guidance

- Either a word processor or a typewriter may be used to complete the exam.

- Stationery: A4 plain paper. Pre-printed templates will be required for those candidates using a typewriter.

- Printing: Candidates **must** carry out their own printing.

- For further information regarding administration for this qualification, please refer to the OCR document *'Administrative Guide for Vocational Qualifications' (A850)*.

Guidance on assessment and evidence requirements

Candidates must produce three business documents to a standard acceptable in the workplace and outcomes must be within the permitted error tolerance.

Penalties are given for errors and the same fault appearing more than once will incur a penalty each time. One fault only will be given to any one word* irrespective of the number of errors that may appear in that word. For example, "miscellaneous" keyed in as "miss-selanious" will be penalised 1 fault, even though several faults have been incurred in the word.

* A word is defined as any normally recognisable word including a hyphenated word and associated punctuation and spacing. Other items that are treated as a word are:

- postcode
- initials and courtesy titles
- simple or complex numbers including money and times
- simple or compound measurements

Invigilators are given clear instructions to report any problems with printers; failure to do so can disadvantage their candidate(s).

You should refer to the *'OCR Administrative Guide to Vocational Qualifications' (A850)* for *Notes on Preventing Computer-Assisted Malpractice*.

Errors will be divided into 4 categories:

Marking Criteria	Tutor Notes
Section 1 Faults - keying in errors **One fault will be given for each word* which:**	
1.1 contains a character which is incorrect (including upper case character within a word), or is illegible for any reason	• A penalty will be incurred for any word that contains a character that is incorrect or that includes an upper case character within a word, eg *LaBel* • Candidates may use English and mother-tongue dictionaries and spellcheckers where available

1.2 has omitted or additional characters or spaces (including omissions caused by faulty use of correction materials/techniques, eg hole in paper)	• A space inserted between a word and its associated punctuation including footnote symbols in text, eg *word ?*, will incure 1 fault per instance • Incorrect or omitted paired punctuation, eg brackets, single quotes, will incur 1 fault per 'pair', eg *(Progress Group)*, ' *Progress Group* ' If footnote symbols omitted altogether and footnote written adjacent to the word which should have contained the symbol – penalise 1 fault for omitted symbol – see also 3.2 (2 faults maximum per instance) • Underlining that is too short or too long (this is not treated as presentation which relates to the underlining of <u>headings</u> – see 4J below)
1.3 contains handwritten character(s)	
1.4 has no space following it	
1.5 has more than 2 character spaces following it, except where appropriate, eg before postcode, after punctuation	In continuous text, 1 fault per instance will be incurred for: • more than 3 spaces appearing after a full stop, question mark, exclamation mark or colon • more than 2 spaces appearing after a comma, semi-colon, closing bracket, dash, apostrophe (at the end of a word) and closing single or double quotes • Where a short line appears, this will be penalised if the first word following could have fitted at the end of the short line with at least 18 mm (¾″) to spare (measuring the short line against the longest line in the document)
1.6 contains overtyping, including overtyping of pre-printed material (per entry regardless of the number of words involved) eg text cutting through letterhead template	

1.7 does not contain initial capitals:
  – as presented in the draft
  – for the first letter of a sentence
	• Candidates should key in text as presented in the draft. One fault per instance will be incurred for each initial capital drafted that has been keyed in as a lower case character
	
	• Failure to insert a capital letter following a penalty for an omitted full stop will not be penalised. Likewise, inserting a capital letter following a penalty for an incorrect full stop will not be penalised

Section 2 Faults - omissions and additions One fault will be given for:	
2.1 each word which is the wrong word or a word that has been omitted or added or not removed as instructed (eg a word which is crossed out in the draft)	This includes: • each omitted and/or additional word which is not required while abstracting information from resource sheet • omitted or additional text resulting from an attempt at vertical or horizontal transposition Letters: • *Our ref* and *Your ref* and reference details must be keyed as shown in the draft, including capitalisation. Treat the whole reference as one unit for marking purposes. Errors in references incur one fault maximum per document, but accept if no linespace between references • Candidates will incur a fault if they set their own reference or omit the reference or add their own initials to the reference • The reference, date, special mark and name and address may be presented in any order but must appear above the salutation and must be keyed in as draft, including capitalisation • The subject heading must appear somewhere between the letterhead details and the first paragraph of the letter and must be keyed in as draft, including capitalisation • Any style of date is acceptable, with the exception of the American numeric format, eg *12/25/2009* as *Christmas Day* • Dates should appear below the letterhead and above the salutation of the letter and should have a clear linespace above/below • Dates wil not be acceptable in the head/footer details alone • One fault will be incurred for each instance of a missing, incomplete or incorrect date to be inserted on correspondence as instructed on the front cover of the question paper • All errors in other dates are penalised per element • Where postdating is required, 1 fault maximum will be incurred for any errors or omissions Fax: • The OCR fax template supplied must be used • Penalise one fault maximum if insertion points (eg *) have been set up but candidate has not deleted them

	• Any style of date is acceptable, with the exception of the American numeric format, eg *12/25/2009* as *Christmas Day*
	• Dates will not be acceptable in the header/footer details alone
	• One fault will be incurred for each instance of a missing, incomplete or incorrect date to be inserted on correspondence as instructed on the front cover of the question paper
	Minutes and Terms of Reference/Contract:
	• If a date appears in a document that does not require dating, this will be penalised 1 fault maximum unless the date appears as part of the personal details or above the first line of the document or below the last line of the document
	Abbreviations:
	• Abbreviations in handwritten draft should be expanded correctly; failure to do so is penalised 1 fault per word (see list in section 3.5)
	NB: commonly used abbreviations must be retained, for example *etc*, *eg*, *ie*, *NB*, *PS*, *plc*, *Ltd* and & in company names
	Footnotes:
	• Accept any symbol, eg * ¹ ʰ etc
	• Symbol in text must match symbol in footnote on same page
	• Footnotes may be displayed with/without space following the footnote symbol (actual footnote at foot of page)
	• Accept any length horizontal line (separator) as part of footnote and accept if footnote is inset
	• If footnotes omitted altogether – penalise 6 faults maximum per document
	• If footnote text appears in body of text and is repeated as a footnote penalise 6 faults maximum per document
	• If footnotes are set up as footers (ie they appear on every page) penalise 6 faults maximum per document
2.2 not applicable to this unit	

2.3 omission of implied or explicit instructions (regardless of the number of words involved) for failure to:
  – insert a subject heading
  – insert a special mark
	• Errors or omissions in a subject heading will incur 1 fault maximum
	
	• Errors or omissions in a special mark will incur 1 fault maximum

- indicate an enclosure - indicate multiple enclosures - underline text - insert page numbers on continuation sheets - rearrange numbered items	• Where enclosures are implied, any appropriate method of indicating them may be used, eg *Enc Att Encs Atts*. Indications must differentiate between single and multiple enclosures • The indication of an enclosure must appear between the signatory details and the footer • Failure to underline a word or words within the text as shown in the draft incurs 1 fault • If page numbers not inserted on continuation sheets, 1 fault maximum is incurred • Page number on page 1 of a multi-page document is acceptable but page numbers on a single-page document will incur a penalty • Page numbers may appear in any position and may be any style but must appear once only on each page of a document • Errors and omissions related to page numbers are limited to 1 fault maximum per exam paper • If numbers in a numbered list are omitted, 1 fault maximum is incurred • If no space is left between the numbers and text in a numbered list, 1 fault maximum is incurred • Numbers may be presented in any style, eg with or without brackets or full stops, inset from left margin • If full stops are inserted at the end of the text where not drafted in a numbered list, 1 fault maximum is incurred (but a full stop following the final item is acceptable) • If underlining is too short or too long, a penalty under 1.2 will be incurred (see 1.2)

Section 3 Faults - transpositions and misplacements
One fault will be given for each instance of:

3.1 items not transposed (horizontally or vertically) in accordance with a correction sign	• Failure to transpose items horizontally or vertically will be penalised 1 fault maximum per correction sign • Where the transposition includes interim text (eg a paragraph or heading between the paragraphs or headings to be transposed) and this is misplaced as a direct result of the attempt to transpose, 1 fault maximum will be incurred
3.2 words that are misplaced within text, where there is no instruction	This includes: • text in columns not aligned horizontally • where footnote does not appear on the same page as the footnote symbol in text • if footnote symbols omitted altogether and footnote written adjacent to the word which should have contained the symbol penalise 1 fault for misplaced text – see also 1.2 (2 faults maximum per instance)

	• where text is inserted more than one linespace above/below pre-printed headings in a fax – penalise up to a maximum of 2 faults per document • transposition of entries against headings in a fax 1 fault each up to a maximum of 2 faults per document
3.3 failure to paragraph as per draft or as specified by a correction sign, eg new paragraph or run on	

Section 4 Faults – presentation
No more than one fault per paper for each of the following items:

4A left, right, top and/or bottom margins of less than 13 mm, or ragged left margin	This includes: • ragged left margin, eg additional character spacing at the beginning of a line or paragraph • main and subheadings not keyed in at the left margin, as presented in draft
4B no clear linespace before and after separate items within a document	This includes: • failure to leave a clear linespace before and after separate items within a document, eg before/after headings, between paragraphs • One-line numbered paragraphs are acceptable in any consistent linespacing, including no clear linespace NB: Where letterhead template is centred or right aligned there is no requirement for a clear linespace below the letterhead. Where the letterhead template is left aligned a clear linespace must be left. No linespace between references is acceptable
4C failure to use linespacing as instructed	This includes: • failure to change linespacing as instructed
4D failure to emphasise text as instructed	This includes: • emphasis extended beyond the required portion • additional emphasis of text where not requested (except for headings – see 4J below) Emphasis may be any method such as bold, italics, underlining, capitals, centring, change of font/size
4E not applicable to this unit	
4F failure to centre text as instructed	• failure to centre text as instructed to within 13 mm over the typing line
4G work which is creased, torn or dirty (including conspicuous corrections)	• Invigilators should report any machine problems resulting in marks on paper • Invigilators should also report any problems with printers, so as not to disadvantage candidates

4H	incorrect stationery used (ie OCR supplied templates, A4 plain paper)	• failure to use OCR supplied templates • The first page of a report may be on plain or letterhead paper • Templates must not be altered in any way
4I	inconsistent spacing between and within similar items within a document	• Inconsistent spacing (including linespacing and spacing between numbers and text in numbered items) between and within similar items is only penalised if a comparison with a similar item can be made within the same document • Inconsistent linespacing above and below an item, for example an inset portion, will not be penalised as there is no further instance of insetting within the same document for comparison

4J	use of initial capitals where not presented in draft, or:
	  – closed capitals used where not presented in draft
	  – failure to use closed capitals as presented in draft
	  – failure to key in headings with initial capitals and underlined as presented in draft
		This includes:
		• use of initial capitals where initial capitals were not presented in draft, eg *Sincerely* in complimentary close
		• closed capitals used where not presented in draft, eg *WHITE* instead of *White*
		• failure to use closed capitals as presented in draft, eg *DISEASES* keyed in as *Diseases*
		• failure to underline headings, including subheadings, as presented in the draft, eg "<u>Miscellaneous Household Items</u>" keyed in as "Miscellaneous Household Items"
		• capitalisation faults in postcodes
		Candidates should key in data exactly as shown in the draft (except for circled words with typographical errors, errors of agreement, punctuation and spelling errors) but additional emboldening, italicising or underlining of headings will not be penalised

4K	inconsistent use of alternative spellings within a document	• Alternative spellings that may be found in an English dictionary will be accepted but a penalty will be incurred if that alternative spelling is used inconsistently, eg *organize* but *organisation* within the same document
4L	inconsistent display of dates, measurements, weights, times, money, figures, dashes/hyphens, lines of ruling within a document	• Dates must be of consistent style throughout a document – for example, if full style is used such as *12 January 2009*, this style should be used for all subsequent dates within the same document (please also refer to Section 2.1 Notes above) • Measurements and weights must be used consistently - for example, *5cm* or *5 cm*; *16kg* or *16 kg* • Times should be keyed in as shown in the draft • Candidates should not change times from 12-hour clock to 24-hour clock or vice versa, unless instructed to do so

	• Money: there must be no character space between £ and the amount, eg £60
	• The display of figures should be an "acceptable system", eg
	  – all figures including "1"
	  – all words (but use of words such as *twenty-five* or *twenty five* must be consistent)
	  – *one* as a word, all others as figures
	  – *one* to *nine* or *ten* as words and then *10* or *11* upwards as figures
	  – *one* to *twenty* as words and then *21* upwards as figures
	• Where dashes or hyphens are used to represent the word "to" (eg *15-22* or *15 – 22*) these must be used consistently throughout a document
	• Any consistent style of numbering paragraphs is acceptable, eg 1 1) 1. (a)

4M inconsistent use of open or full punctuation within a document	This includes: • a full stop appearing in any abbreviation such as enc, cc, eg, am, when open punctuation has been used • a missing full stop in any abbreviation such as enc., c.c., e.g., a.m., where full punctuation has been used
4N insertion of an additional comma which alters the meaning of a sentence	• Candidates should key in punctuation as presented in the draft • The insertion of an additional comma will only be penalised if this alters the meaning of the sentence
4P failure to align column headings and text in columns to the left consistently	
4Q not applicable to this unit	
4R not applicable to this unit	
4S not applicable to this unit	
4T not applicable to this unit	
4U failure to inset from left margin as instructed	• The inset measurement must be exactly as instructed • If extra text has been incorrectly included within the insetting, a penalty will be incurred • Text inserted from the right margin as well as the left margin will incur a penalty

RECOGNISING ACHIEVEMENT

TEXT PROCESSING (BUSINESS PROFESSIONAL)

Word Processing
03938

Level:	3
Credits:	6
Learning Time:	60 hours

Learning outcomes	Assessment criteria	Knowledge, understanding and skills
1 Use a word processor efficiently	1.1 Use the different functions of a word processor	• Change left and right margins • Use full justification • Change linespacing • Underline text • Centre text • Set and change font style and size • Pagination • Number pages with page numbers specified • Insert a header and a footer with position and font specified • Advanced Search and Replace • Move and copy text within the same document • Copy text to a separate document • Insert a text box of specific size with text wrapped as specified • Inset text from left and right margins • Present information in columns of specified width • Use track changes to display alterations • Produce a complex table with horizontal and vertical headings • Sort data • Align decimal points • Produce a two-sided booklet style document • Insert and re-size a picture • Use spellchecker • Print using portrait and landscape

Learning outcomes	Assessment criteria	Knowledge, understanding and skills
2 Input text from handwritten and typewritten drafts and information given on a resource sheet	2.1 Produce text accurately and efficiently, using a variety of fonts, from handwritten and typewritten drafts and print as instructed	• Plan and organise work within deadlines • Read and transcribe variable quality manuscript • Plan layout of work in a variety of formats • Accurately key in text from handwritten and typewritten drafts and from a resource sheet • Use consistent style and format of presentation with at least one clear linespace before and after separate items within a document • Use plain A4 paper • Use English and mother-tongue dictionaries • Interpret written instructions • Check accuracy of amendments and that all instructions have been carried out correctly • Use spellcheckers • Proofread and correct errors
3 Produce four business documents (totalling no more than 1215 words – 600 to be input and no more than 615 words to be recalled) in the time allowed (1 hour 45 minutes)	3.1 Recall a multi-page report/article, amend and print as instructed	• Recall text from pre-stored file retaining font style and size • Adjust left and right margins as instructed • Change text to full justification throughout the document • Move two sections of text to two separate positions • Copy one section of text to two separate positions • Remove page breaks • Insert new page breaks as appropriate to ensure widow/orphan control • Insert a header using a specified font style and size and in a specified position • Insert a footer using a specified font style and size and in a specified position • Number pages as specified

Learning outcomes	Assessment criteria	Knowledge, understanding and skills
		• Advanced Search and Replace matching case as draft, or whole word • Case change • Allocation of vertical and horizontal space by inserting a text box of specific size and wrapping text around the box as instructed • Sort a list alphabetically or chronologically • Use single and double linespacing • Inset a section of text from left and right margins • Print document on plain A4 paper

	3.2 Amend text as instructed	• Amend text as shown in draft:
		  – deletion with replacement words
		  – deletion without replacement words
		Follow correction signs:
		New paragraph ⌐ or ∥
		Run on ∽
		Insertion with word(s) above ∧ or balloon with arrow
		Transpose horizontally ∼ or balloon with arrow eg
		Transpose vertically
		– transpose consecutive items vertically
		Close up ◡
		Leave a space /
		Stet – – – – – with ✓ in margin

	3.3 Recall a newspaper style article/information sheet, amend and print as instructed	• Recall text from pre-stored file retaining font style and size and full justification • Produce a document in columns of specified width • Ensure left, right, top and bottom margins are at least 13 mm • Make alterations displaying track changes

Learning outcomes	Assessment criteria	Knowledge, understanding and skills
		<ul><li>Incorporate appropriate text from a resource sheet as instructed</li><li>Print one copy of the document on plain A4 paper displaying the track changes</li><li>Print a second copy of the document on plain A4 paper with all editing changes accepted</li></ul>
	3.4 Key in a table (which may include continuous text) from handwritten and typewritten draft and print as instructed	<ul><li>Ensure left, right, top and bottom margins are at least 13 mm</li><li>Key in a table using a specified font style and size from handwritten and typewritten drafts. The ruling of the table must be carried out on a word processor</li><li>Key in four columns (one sub-divided) with multi-line headings and three sections of data containing text and numbers</li><li>Display horizontal and vertical column headings as indicated</li><li>Key in a main heading and column headings in capitals</li><li>Ensure data in columns and column headings are left aligned consistently</li><li>Ensure decimal points are aligned consistently and that the longest figure Is left aligned with the column heading</li><li>Incorporate data from a resource sheet to complete the table as instructed</li><li>Carry out two aspects of modification, eg change the sequence of columns and change the order of sections</li><li>Sort columns as instructed numerically or chronologically</li></ul>

Learning outcomes	Assessment criteria	Knowledge, understanding and skills
		• Print one copy of the document on plain A4 portrait • Follow instructions on a resource sheet to carry out two further aspects of modification, eg add shading as specified, remove text or lines as specified, change the style of lines • Print a second copy of the document on plain A4 portrait
	3.5 Key in a two-sided booklet/programme/ leaflet style document from handwritten and typewritten drafts and print as instructed	• Ensure left, right, top and bottom margins around all pages are at least 13 mm • Format document for landscape printing • Key in leaflet from handwritten and typewritten drafts using a specified font style and size • Centre one or more lines of text as specified • Underline words which will be included in handwritten text in the draft • Copy part of a pre-stored document as specified ensuring consistency of font style and size with the main document • Insert a picture (one of three to be provided by OCR) and re-size as instructed • Use emphasis by changing the font style and size for one portion of text as instructed • Print document on one or two sheets of plain A4 landscape

Unit aim

This unit aims to equip candidates with the ability to produce, from handwritten and typewritten draft material, recalled text and supplementary information, using a word processor, a variety of complex and/or specialist business documents to a standard that meets the requirements of employment.

Assessment

Assessment will consist of producing four business documents totalling no more than 1215 words (600 words to be input by candidates and no more than 615 recalled words) and will take the form of a 1 hour 45 minute test set and marked by OCR.

Results will be graded Distinction, Pass or Fail.

To achieve a Distinction, candidates must produce the documents with no more than 5 faults within the time allowed (1 hour 45 minutes).

To achieve a Pass, candidates must produce the documents with no more than 14 faults within the time allowed (1 hour 45 minutes).

The grade achieved will be stated on the certificate.

Administration guidance

- Word processing equipment **must** be used to complete the exam

- Centres must ensure that the recall material for this examination is available for candidates. This recall material will be available on CD-ROM provided by OCR or can be downloaded from Interchange, OCR's secure website. A variety of fonts will be used – Tahoma, Courier New, Arial, Times New Roman, Comic Sans MS, Trebuchet MS, Century Gothic

- Centres must ensure that the above fonts are available

- Centres **must not** re-key or amend the pre-stored documents

- Stationery: A4 plain paper will be required

- Printing: Candidates **must** carry out their own printing

- For further information regarding administration for this qualification, please refer to the OCR document 'Administrative Guide for Vocational Qualifications' (A850).

Guidance on assessment and evidence requirements

Candidates must produce four business documents to a standard acceptable in the workplace and outcomes must be within the permitted error tolerance.

Penalties are given for errors and the same fault appearing more than once will incur a penalty each time. One fault only will be given to any one word* irrespective of the number of errors that may appear in that word. For example, "miscellaneous" keyed in as "miss-selanious" will be penalised 1 fault, even though several faults have been incurred in the word.

* A word is defined as any normally recognisable word including a hyphenated word and associated punctuation and spacing. Other items that are treated as a word are:

- postcode
- initials and courtesy titles
- simple or complex numbers including money and times
- simple or compound measurements

You should refer to the *'OCR Administrative Guide to Vocational Qualifications' (A850)* for *Notes on Preventing Computer-Assisted Malpractice*

Errors will be divided into 4 categories:

Marking Criteria	Tutor Notes
Section 1 Faults - keying in errors **One fault will be given for each word* which:**	
1.1 contains a character which is incorrect (including upper case character within a word), or is illegible for any reason	• A penalty will be incurred for any word that contains a character that is incorrect or that includes an upper case character within a word, eg *LaBel* • Candidates may use English and mother-tongue dictionaries and spellcheckers where available
1.2 has omitted or additional characters or spaces (including omissions caused by faulty use of correction materials/techniques)	• A space inserted between a word and its associated punctuation, eg *word :* or *word ?*, will incur 1 fault per instance • Incorrect or omitted paired punctuation, eg brackets, single quotes, will incur 1 fault per pair, eg (*Progress Group*), ' *Progress Group* '
1.3 contains handwritten character(s)	• Ruling of the table must be carried out on a word processor
1.4 has no space following it	
1.5 has more than 2 character spaces following it, except where appropriate, eg before postcode, after punctuation	• In continuous text, 1 fault per instance will be incurred for: – more than 3 spaces appearing after a full stop, question mark, exclamation mark or colon – more than 2 spaces appearing after a comma, semi-colon, closing bracket, dash, apostrophe (at the end of a word) and closing single or double quotes – where a short line appears, this will be penalised if the first word following could have fitted at the end of the short line with at least 18 mm (¾") to spare (measuring the short line against the longest line in the document)
1.6 contains overtyping, including overtyping of pre-printed material (per entry regardless of the number of words involved)	
1.7 does not contain initial capitals as presented in the draft, including the first letter of a sentence	• Candidates should key in text as presented in the draft. One fault per instance will be incurred for each initial capital drafted that has been keyed in as a lower case character • Failure to insert a capital letter following a penalty for an omitted full stop will not be penalised

Marking Criteria	Tutor Notes
	• Inserting a capital letter following a penalty for an incorrect full stop will not be penalised
	• With case change where capitals are to be changed to lower case, a penalty will be taken if there is no initial capital at the beginning of the sentence
Section 2 Faults – omissions and additions **One fault will be given for:**	
2.1 each word which is the wrong word and a word that has been omitted or added or not removed as instructed (eg a word which is crossed out in the draft)	• Failure to delete recalled text and insert replacement words will incur 1 fault per wrong word or for each word that has been omitted
	• The unspecified deletion and/or duplication of recalled text will incur 1 fault per word, unless it can be attributed to a vertical or horizontal transposition, deletion without replacement (NB see 2.2 below), move or copy
	• All errors in other dates are penalised per element
	• Any style of date is acceptable, with the exception of the American numerical format, eg *12/25/2008* as *Christmas Day*
	• If a date appears in a document that does not require dating, this will be penalised 1 fault max unless the date appears as part of the personal details
	• Incorporation of information from a resource sheet will be penalised 1 fault per omitted or additional word
	• If a vertical or horizontal transposition includes an amendment to text (eg deletion with replacement words) or a correction sign for insertion of words (caret sign, balloon or "stet"), 1 fault per word for wrong/omitted words will be incurred (see also 3.1)
	• Any omitted, additional or incorrect words in a list to be sorted will be penalised 1 fault per word
	• Errors in text within a text box will be penalised 1 fault per word
2.2 – each instance of failure to delete recalled text as instructed – each instance of failure to print a second copy of a document as specified	• Failure to delete recalled text as shown in the draft will incur 1 fault maximum This relates to deletions where there are no replacement words written above the words crossed through irrespective of the number of words involved

Marking Criteria	Tutor Notes
2.3 omission of implied or explicit instructions (regardless of the number of words involved) for failure to: – ensure consistent use of font style/size throughout a document – change the font style/size as instructed – insert a header as instructed – insert a footer as instructed – number pages as specified – delete page breaks – insert page breaks as appropriate, extending continuous text (including headings) to at least two lines at the bottom and top of every page to enable widow/orphan control – carry out an aspect of modification as instructed (this includes each modification to the table, Search and Replace and case conversion) – insert a text box of specific size with text wrapping around as instructed – indicate track changes – insert and re-size a picture as instructed – underline text – insert a table as draft – produce a document in columns of specified width – produce a booklet-style document as draft	• Changes made to the font style/size throughout a document where there is no instruction to do so will incur 1 fault maximum per paper • Failure to use a specific font style/size as instructed will incur 1 fault maximum per document • Failure to insert a header or a footer using a specified font style and size and in the specified positions incurs 1 fault maximum per header and 1 fault maximum per footer (including keying errors). Headers and footers may appear within the margin allowance (see also 4J) • Errors and omissions related to page numbers are limited to 1 fault maximum per exam paper • Failure to insert page numbers as instructed incurs 1 fault maximum • Insertion of page numbers on single-page documents incurs 1 fault maximum • Page numbers may appear in any position and may be any style but must appear once only on each page of a document • In the multi-page document, page breaks in recalled text must be deleted and appropriate page breaks must be inserted to ensure widow/orphan control. Incorrect pagination will incur 1 fault maximum • Failure to carry out an aspect of modification, eg change the sequence of columns in a table, will incur 1 fault • The word used in Search and Replace will not be presented consistently, eg, SHARE, Share, share. Words should be replaced matching case as shown in the draft. Failure to replace one or all instances will be penalised 1 fault maximum • Errors and omissions relating to the insertion of a text box as instructed will be penalised 4 faults maximum • The text box must be centred horizontally within a section of text as instructed, with text wrapping around the box on all sides. (See also 2.1, 4E and 4R) • Failure to accurately centre the text box horizontally will incur 1 fault • Text in text box does not need to be centred • Failure to wrap the text as instructed will incur 1 fault • Track changes must be indicated as instructed on one document. Failure to show/remove track changes will incur 1 fault maximum • Failure to print a second copy showing/removing track changes will be penalised 2 faults maximum (1 fault under 2.2 for failure to print a second copy and 1 fault under 2.3 for failure to show/remove track changes)

Marking Criteria	Tutor Notes
	• Failure to produce a document in columns of specified width will incur 1 fault maximum. Column width must be exact
	• The picture to be inserted will be one of three provided by OCR on disk. Failure to insert the correct picture and/or re-size as instructed will incur 2 faults maximum. Measurements of the picture must be accurate within a 1 mm tolerance
	• Failure to underline a word or words within the text exactly as shown in the draft incurs 1 fault maximum, including omission of the underline and underlining which is too long or too short
	• Column headings in the table must be as draft and display of data will be indicated on a resource sheet
	• Any additional or omitted lines of ruling will be penalised 1 fault maximum
	• Failure to leave a character space between text and vertical lines of ruling <u>in the table</u> will not be penalised
	• Incorrect splitting of words, without hyphen, caused by word wrapping at the end of column will be penalised 1 fault maximum
	• Failure to print a second copy of the table will be penalised 3 faults maximum (1 fault under 2.2 for failure to print a second copy and 2 faults under 2.3 for failure to carry out 2 modifications)
	• The booklet-style document must be displayed as draft and may be printed on 1 sheet of A4 plain landscape (double-sided) or on 2 sheets of A4 plain landscape if double-sided printing is not available (NB see also 3.2). The pages should not be numbered
Section 3 Faults - transpositions and misplacements	
One fault will be given for each instance of:	
3.1 items not transposed (horizontally or vertically) in accordance with a correction sign	• Failure to transpose items (horizontally or vertically) in accordance with an amendment sign will incur 1 fault (see also 2.1)
	• Words that have been omitted as a direct result of incorrect horizontal or vertical transposition of recalled text are penalised 1 fault maximum
	• If interim text (and/or other associated text) is misplaced, ie it is no longer positioned between paragraphs or headings to be vertically transposed, no further penalty will be incurred, other than the 1 fault already incurred for failure to transpose the paragraphs as instructed, as the misplacement is a direct result of an attempt to transpose text vertically

Marking Criteria	Tutor Notes
3.2 words that are misplaced within text, where there is no instruction	• Failure to align data horizontally in the table will be penalised 1 fault maximum • Failure to follow layout of text in booklet style document as shown in draft will be penalised 1 fault maximum
3.3 failure to paragraph as per draft or as specified by a correction sign, eg new paragraph or run on	
3.4 a list of items not sorted as instructed	• Failure to sort a list as instructed will incur 1 fault maximum • Failure to ensure that corresponding details are correctly rearranged in the table sort will incur 1 fault maximum • Any omitted, additional or incorrect words in a list to be sorted will be penalised 1 fault per word

3.5 failure to copy text as instructed	• 1 fault maximum will be incurred for:
	  – failure to copy text within a document as instructed
	  – failure to copy text from another document as instructed
	  – copying the wrong text
	  – moving the text rather than copying text
	  – if all or part of the text to be copied is duplicated or missing

3.6 failure to move text as instructed	• 1 fault maximum per instance will be incurred for:
	  – failure to move text as instructed
	  – moving the wrong text
	  – copying text rather than moving text
	  – if all or part of the text to be moved is duplicated or missing

Section 4 Faults – presentation	
No more than one fault per paper for each of the following items:	
4A left, right, top and bottom margins of less than 13 mm (unless otherwise instructed), or ragged left margin	• Ragged left margin, eg additional character spacing at the beginning of a line or paragraph • Main and subheadings not keyed in at the left margin, as presented in draft – unless otherwise instructed (eg centring) or recalled • Section headings in table must appear as draft • When the booklet/programme/leaflet is folded, the margins around <u>all</u> pages must be a minimum of 13 mm
4B no clear linespace before and after separate items within a document	• Failure to leave a clear linespace before and after separate items within a document, eg before/after headings, between paragraphs • Failure to leave a clear linespace between the main heading and the table and after any sub-headings within the table

Marking Criteria	Tutor Notes
4C failure to use linespacing as instructed	• Failure to change linespacing as instructed
4D failure to emphasise text as instructed	• Emphasis to be by change of font style and size only • Emphasis extended beyond the required portion • Additional emphasis of text where not requested • Failure to clearly change the font or size of some text as instructed will incur a penalty. Note that if the changes are not clear, eg using similar sans serif fonts or changing the font size by one point, a penalty will be incurred
4E allocation of space not as instructed	• Measurements of the text box must be accurate (see also 2.3)
4F failure to centre text or data as instructed	
4G work which is creased, torn or dirty (including conspicuous corrections)	• Invigilators must notify OCR of any machine faults resulting in marks on the paper • Invigilators should also report any problems with printers, so as not to disadvantage candidates
4H incorrect stationery used (ie A4 plain paper, portrait/landscape)	• Failure to use landscape/portrait where instructed
4I inconsistent spacing between and within similar items within a document	• Inconsistent spacing (including linespacing) between and within similar items is only penalised if a comparison with a similar item can be made within the same document Inconsistent linespacing above and below an item, for example an inset portion, will not be penalised as there is no further instance of insetting within the same document for comparsion

4J use of initial capitals where not presented in draft, or:
  – closed capitals used where not presented in draft
  – failure to use closed capitals as presented in draft
  – failure to key in headings with initial capitals and underlined as presented in draft
  – failure to follow capitalisation in headers and footers as presented in draft (see also 2.3)
	This includes:
	• Use of initial capitals where initial capitals were not presented in draft
	• Closed capitals used where not presented in draft, eg *White* keyed in as *WHITE*
	• Failure to use closed capitals as presented in draft, eg *DISEASES* keyed in as *Diseases*
	• Failure to underline headings, including subheadings, as presented in the draft, eg "<u>Miscellaneous Household Items</u>" keyed in as "Miscellaneous Household Items"
	• Capitalisation faults in postcodes
	• Candidates should key in data exactly as shown in the draft but additional emboldening, italicising or underlining of headings will not be penalised

4K inconsistent use of alternative spellings within a document	• Alternative spellings that may be found in an English dictionary will be accepted but a penalty will be incurred if that alternative spelling is used inconsistently, eg *organize* but *organisation* within the same document

4L	inconsistent display of dates, measurements, weights, times, money, figures, dashes/hyphens, lines of ruling within a document	• Dates must be of consistent style throughout a document. For example, if full style is used, such as *12 January 2008*, this style should be used for all subsequent dates within the same document
		• Measurements and weights must be used consistently. For example, *5 cm* or *5cm*; *16 kg* or *16kg*
		• Times should be keyed in as shown in the draft. Times must be keyed in consistently within a document eg *10.30am* and *2.30 pm* within the same document would incur a penalty. Candidates must ensure that times that they key in are consistent with those that appear in recalled text within a document. Candidates must not change times from 12-hour clock to 24-hour clock or vice versa unless instructed to do so
		• Money: there must be no character space between £ and the amount, eg *£60*. In columns and tables accept spacing between £ and amount
		• Numbers with multiple digits can be keyed in with or without a comma, eg *10,000* or *10000*, but must be consistent. *10 000* is not acceptable
		• The display of figures should be an "acceptable system", eg
		– all figures including "1"
		– all words (but use of words such as *twenty-five* or *twenty five* must be consistent)
		– *one* as a word, all others as figures
		– *one* to *nine* or *ten* as words and then *10* or *11* upwards as figures
		– *one* to *twenty* as words and then *21* upwards as figures
		• Where dashes or hyphens are used to represent the word "to" (eg *15-22* or *15 – 22*) these must be used consistently throughout a document
4M	inconsistent use of open or full punctuation within a document	• Abbreviations may be keyed in with open punctuation (*eg*, *am*, *pm*) or with full punctuation (*e.g.*, *a.m.*, *p.m.*) but must be consistent
4N	insertion of an additional comma which alters the meaning of a sentence	• Candidates should key in punctuation as presented in the draft. However, the insertion of an additional comma will only be penalised if this alters the meaning of the sentence
4O	not applicable to this unit	
4P	– failure to align text and figures in columns to the left consistently	
	– failure to align data in columns consistently with column headings	

4Q	failure to align the decimal points in column of numbers	• In addition to the correct alignment of decimal points, the first figure of the longest amount in each column should be left-aligned with the column heading
4R	failure to leave at least one clear space between vertical ruled lines and text	• This applies only to the text box

4S	failure to justify text or data as instructed	• A penalty will be incurred:
		  – where right margin justification requested but left margin is ragged
		  – if justification is lost on last line of page
		  – if justification used when a right ragged margin is requested
		  – if full justification is not retained in a recalled document as instructed

4T	failure to adjust margins or line length as instructed	Left and right margins must be adjusted as instructed within a 3 mm tolerance
4U	failure to inset from left margin as instructed	• The inset measurement must be exact. If extra text has been incorrectly included within the insetting, a penalty will be incurred • Insetting the wrong section of text incurs 1 fault maximum
4V	failure to inset from right margin as instructed	• The inset measurement must be exactly as instructed. If extra text has been incorrectly included within the insetting, a penalty will be incurred • Insetting the wrong section of text incurs 1 fault maximum
4W	failure to display vertical headings as indicated in draft	• Vertical headings in the table must be displayed as VERTICAL

TEXT PROCESSING (BUSINESS PROFESSIONAL)

Audio-Transcription

03933

Level:	3
Credits:	5
Learning Time:	50 hours

Learning outcomes	Assessment criteria	Knowledge, understanding and skills
1 Use audio equipment, word processor or a typewriter effectively	1.1 Use the different functions of a word processor or different parts of the typewriter in co-ordination with audio equipment	• Set top and left margins of at least 13 mm • Alter linespacing (single/double) as instructed • Emphasise text as instructed, eg emboldening, underlining, capitals, etc • Interpreting dictated text, eg knowledge of English grammar and spelling. Use of spellchecker, understanding homophones, etc • Understanding of verbal instructions for punctuation, eg full stop (.) comma (,) oblique (/) etc
2 Enter and format text from recorded material	2.1 Produce text accurately and efficiently from Information Sheet and recorded material	• Plan and organise work within deadlines • Plan layout of work in a variety of formats • Accurately key in text from recorded speech • Interpret audio instructions • Proofread and correct errors, using appropriate correction techniques, to ensure work is 100% accurate • Use consistent style and format of presentation with at least one clear linespace before and after separate items within a document • Use appropriate stationery

		• Use English and mother-tongue dictionaries • Check accuracy of amendments and that all instructions have been carried out correctly
3 Produce business documents	3.1 Key in and print a business letter on a pre-printed letterhead or by use of a template from recorded material	• Use conventional and consistent layout and style of a business letter • Use OCR supplied letterhead template • *Our ref* and *Your ref* details (if used) are keyed in as shown on the information sheet, including capitalisation • Insert today's date on letter • Insert a special mark, as dictated, eg *Private and Confidential*, *Urgent* etc • Insert a subject heading as dictated • Indicate enclosure(s), as implied in the verbal instruction, using an acceptable convention • Produce extra copies and indicate routing on each copy. Destination details must be presented on the top and subsequent copies
	3.2 Key in and print minutes, advertisement or itinerary from recorded material	• Use conventional and consistent layout and style of a variety of business documents • Insert headings as dictated • Emphasise text, eg emboldening, underlining, capitals • Centre over the typing line • Allocate vertical space as instructed

	3.3 Key in and print an article or report from recorded material	• Use conventional and consistent layout and style of a report or article • Insert a page number on continuation sheets • Use single/double linespacing as instructed • Insert a subject heading as dictated • Insert subheadings as instructed • Key in a table as dictated • Change linespacing as instructed • Produce numbered paragraphs or items as instructed • Include distraction element
	3.4 Amend word corrections as dictated	
	3.5 Insert a table within text	• Key in a table from recorded speech • Key in three or four columns of data containing text and numbers • Ensure data in columns and column headings are aligned consistently

Unit aim

This unit aims to equip candidates with the ability to produce a variety of routine business documents to a standard that meets the business document production requirements of employment from recorded speech and information provided on the information sheet.

Assessment

Assessment will consist of producing three business documents totalling 900 words and will take the form of a 1 hour 30 minute test set and marked by OCR.

In order to subject the candidates to distraction, extra details for Document 3 will be announced by the Invigilator approximately 15-30 minutes after the start of work.

Candidates will be required to work from recorded speech containing interpolations and corrections to produce 3 documents. The dictation will be given by means of a recording played on equipment over which the candidates have individual control.

Results will be graded Distinction, Pass or Fail.

To achieve a Distinction, candidates must produce the documents with no more than 4 faults within the time allowed (1 hour 30 minutes).

To achieve a Pass, candidates must produce the documents with no more than 11 faults within the time allowed (1 hour 30 minutes).

The grade achieved will be stated on the certificate.

Administration guidance

- Either a word processor or a typewriter may be used to complete the exam

- Dictation for Audio-Transcription is recorded and supplied by OCR as mp3 and .wav files on CD-ROM and downloadable from OCR Interchange. The material must be copied onto equipment over which the candidates have individual control

- Stationery: A4 plain paper. Pre-printed templates will be required for those candidates using a typewriter

- Printing: Candidates **must** carry out their own printing. (Photocopying may be undertaken by an appointed person but routing must be undertaken by the candidate)

- Audio equipment to be supplied by the Centre

- For further information regarding administration for this qualification, please refer to the OCR document '*Administrative Guide for Vocational Qualifications*' (A850)

Guidance on assessment and evidence requirements

Candidates must produce three business documents to a standard acceptable in the workplace and outcomes must be within the permitted error tolerance.

Penalties are given for errors and the same fault appearing more than once will incur a penalty each time. One fault only will be given to any one word* irrespective of the number of errors that may appear in that word. For example "miscellaneous" keyed in as "miss-selanious" will be penalised 1 fault, even though several faults have been incurred in the word.

* A word is defined as any normally recognisable word including a hyphenated word and associated punctuation and spacing. Other items that are treated as a word are:

- postcode
- initials and courtesy titles
- simple or complex numbers including money, times and telephone numbers
- simple or compound measurements

You should refer to the '*OCR Administrative Guide to Vocational Qualifications (A850)*' for *Notes on Preventing Computer-Assisted Malpractice.*

Errors will be divided into 4 categories:

Marking criteria	Tutor Notes
Section 1 Faults – keying in errors	
One fault will be given for each word* which:	
1.1 contains a character which is incorrect (including upper case character within a word), or is illegible for any reason	• A penalty will be incurred for any word that contains a character that is incorrect or that includes an upper case character within a word, eg *LaBel* • Candidates may use English and mother-tongue dictionaries and spellcheckers where available
1.2 has omitted or additional characters or spaces (including omissions caused by faulty use of correction materials/techniques, eg hole in paper)	• A space inserted between a word and its associated punctuation, eg *word :* or *word ?*, will incur 1 fault per instance • Incorrect or omitted paired punctuation, eg brackets, single quotes, will incur 1 fault per 'pair', eg *(Progress Group)*, ' *Progress Group* '
1.3 contains handwritten character(s)	
1.4 has no space following it	
1.5 has more than 2 character spaces following it, except where appropriate, eg before postcode, after punctuation	In continuous text, 1 fault per instance will be incurred for: • more than 3 spaces appearing after a full stop, question mark, exclamation mark or colon • more than 2 spaces appearing after a comma, semi-colon, closing bracket, dash, apostrophe (at the end of a word) and closing single or double quotes • Where a short line appears, this will be penalised if the first word following could have fitted at the end of the short line with at least 18 mm (¾") to spare (measuring the short line against the longest line in the document)
1.6 contains overtyping, including overtyping of pre-printed material (per entry regardless of the number of words involved), eg text cutting through letterhead template	

1.7 does not contain initial capitals:
  – as presented on the information sheet
  – for the first letter of a sentence
	• Candidates should key in text as dictated. One fault per instance will be incurred for each initial capital presented on the information sheet that has been keyed in as a lower case character
	
	• Initial capitals will not be dictated for proper nouns or at the beginning of sentences. One fault per instance will be incurred for each initial capital that has been keyed in as a lower case character for proper nouns or at the beginning of a sentence

	• Failure to insert a capital letter following a penalty for an omitted full stop will not be penalised. Likewise, inserting a capital letter following a penalty for an incorrect full stop will not be penalised
Section 2 Faults – omissions and additions	
One fault will be given for:	
2.1 each word which is the wrong word and a word that that has been omitted or added	• Any style of *Our ref* is acceptable, but candidates will incur a fault if they set up their own reference (not as dictated or on the information sheet), or omit the reference, or add their own initials to the reference
	• The reference(s), date, name and address may be presented in any order but must appear above the salutation and must be keyed in as given on the information sheet, including capitalisation
	• The subject heading must appear somewhere between the letterhead details and the first paragraph of the letter and must be keyed in as dictated
	• Any style of date is acceptable, with the exception of the American numerical format, eg *12/25/2009* as *Christmas Day*
	• Dates should appear below the letterhead and above the salutation of the letter and should have a clear linespace above/below
	• Dates will not be acceptable in the header/footer details alone
	• One fault will be incurred for each instance of a missing, incomplete or incorrect date to be inserted on correspondence as instructed on the front cover of the question paper
	• All errors in other dates are penalised per element
	• Where postdating is required, one fault maximum will be incurred for any errors or omissions
	• If a date appears in a document that does not require dating, this will be penalised 1 fault max unless the date appears as part of the personal details or above the first line of the document or below the last line of the document

2.2
 	
  - failure to indicate routing as dictated
  - failure to produce an extra copy
	• Two extra copies must be produced, either by photocopying, additional printouts or from typewriter memory
	
	• Failure to produce extra copies will be penalised 1 fault per copy missing

	• Errors relating to extra copies, such as errors, omissions in destination details, or incorrect or omitted routing are limited to 2 faults maximum
	• Copies may be produced on OCR template or plain A4 paper, if using a typewriter

2.3 omission of implied or explicit instructions (regardless of the number of words involved) for failure to:
 	
   – insert a subject heading
   – insert a special mark eg Private and Confidential, Urgent
   – indicate an enclosure
   – insert page numbers on continuation sheet
   – indicate additional destination on all copies
   – indicate routing on appropriate extra copy
	• Errors or omissions in a subject heading will incur 1 fault max

	• Errors or omissions in a special mark will incur 1 fault max
	• Where enclosures are implied, any method of indicating them may be used, eg *Enc, Att, Encs, Atts*. Indications must differentiate between single and multiple enclosures
	• The indication of an enclosure must appear between the signatory details and the footer
	• Page number on page 1 of a multi-page document is acceptable but page numbers on a single-page document will incur a penalty
	• Page numbers may appear in any position and may be any style but must appear once only on each page of a document
	• Errors and omissions related to page numbers are limited to 1 fault max per exam paper
	• If numbers in a numbered list are omitted, 1 fault max is incurred
	• The destination details must appear on all copies of the letter. These may include "file" or "files"
	• The destination details must include the word "copy" "cc" or similar – if not, 1 fault will be incurred
	• If addressee's name is included in destination details, 1 fault max will be incurred
	• Any method of indication of routing will be accepted, eg "tick", special mark or character, emphasis such as bold, underline or use of highlighter pen
	• Indicate special mark as instructed

Section 3 Faults – transpositions and misplacements	
One fault will be given for each instance of:	
3.1 not applicable to this unit	
3.2 words that are misplaced within text, where there is no instruction	This includes: • words inserted in the wrong order or place in the absence of an instruction, eg misplaced within text or as foot or marginal note, regardless of the amount of material involved (in addition to any faults that may be incurred above) • in a memo, transposition of entries against "To, From" headings incurs 1 fault per misplaced item
3.3 failure to paragraph as per verbal instruction	

Section 4 Faults – presentation	
No more than one fault per paper for each of the following items:	
4A left and/or top margins of less than 13 mm, or ragged left margin	This includes: • ragged left margin, eg additional character spacing at the beginning of a line or paragraph • main and sub-headings not keyed in at the left margin in the absence of an alternative instruction
4B no clear linespace before and after separate items within a document	• Failure to leave a clear linespace before and after separate items within a document, eg before/after headings, between paragraphs • One-line numbered paragraphs are acceptable with any consistent linespacing, including no clear linespacing NB: Where letterhead template is centred or right aligned there is no requirement for a clear linespace below the letterhead. Where the letterhead template is left aligned a clear linespace must be left
4C failure to use linespacing as instructed	This includes: • failure to change linespacing as instructed • accept one clear line space after heading before table text in single linespacing • accept one, two or three single line spaces before table text in double line spacing.
4D failure to emphasise text as instructed	This includes: • emphasis extended beyond the required portion • additional emphasis of text where not requested (except for headings see 4.I below) • emphasis may be any method such as bold, italics or underlining

4E allocation of space not as instructed	
4F failure to centre text or data as instructed	• Failure to centre text or data as instructed to within 13 mm over the typing line
4G work which is creased, torn or dirty (including conspicuous corrections)	• Errors on copies that did not appear on the top copy will be penalised under 4G • Invigilators should report any machine problems resulting in marks on paper • Invigilators should also report any problems with printers, so as not to disadvantage the candidates
4H incorrect stationery used (ie letterhead, A4 plain paper)	• The first page of a report may be produced on plain or headed paper • Failure to use OCR templates • Templates must not be altered in any way
4I inconsistent spacing between and within similar items within a document	• Inconsistent spacing (including linespacing) between and within similar items is only penalised if a comparison with a similar item can be made within the same document
	• Inconsistent linespacing above and below an item, for example, the table, will not be penalised as there is no further instance of a table within the same document for comparison

4J use of initial capitals where not presented on the information sheet, or:
  - closed capitals used where not dictated
  - failure to use closed capitals as dictated
  - failure to key in headings with initial capitals and underline as dictated
	This includes:
	• use of initial capitals where initial capitals were not dictated eg *Sincerely* in complimentary close
	
	• headings with initial capitals are acceptable as: *Facilities in all Conference Rooms*, or *Facilities In All Conference Rooms*
	
	• closed capitals where not dictated or presented on the information sheet, eg *White* keyed in as *WHITE*
	
	• failure to use closed capitals as dictated eg *DISEASES* keyed in as *Diseases*
	
	• failure to underline headings, including subheadings, as dictated, eg "<u>Miscellaneous Household Items</u>" keyed in as "Miscellaneous Household Items"
	
	• capitalisation faults in postcodes and references
	
	• Candidates should key in data exactly as dictated and as given on the information sheet but additional emboldening, italicising or underlining of headings will not be penalised

4K inconsistent use of alternative spellings within a document	• Alternative spellings that may be found in an English dictionary will be accepted but a penalty will be incurred if that alternative spelling is used inconsistently, eg *organize* but *organisation* within the same document
4L inconsistent display of dates, measurements, weights, times, money, figures, dashes/hyphens, lines of ruling within a document	• Dates must be of consistent style throughout a document. For example, if full style is used, such as *12 January 2009*, this style should be used for all subsequent dates within the same document. (Please also refer to Section (2.1) Notes above) • Measurements and weights must be used consistently. For example, *5 cm* or *5cm*; *16 kg* or *16kg* • Times should be keyed in as dictated. Candidates should not change times from 12-hour clock to 24-hour clock or vice versa, unless instructed to do so

	• Money; there must be no character space between £ and the amount, eg *£60*. However, in columns and tables accept spacing between £ and amount
	
	• The display of figures should be an "acceptable system", eg
	   - all figures including "*1*"
	   - all words (but use of words such as *twenty-five* or *twenty five* must be (consistent)
	   - *one* as a word, all others as figures
	   - *one* to *nine* or *ten* as words and *10* or *11* upwards as figures
	   - *one* to *twenty* as words and then *21* upwards as figures
	
	• Where dashes or hyphens are used to represent the word "to" (eg *15-22* or *15 - 22*) these must be used consistently throughout a document
	
	• Lines of ruling in a table – a candidate opting to use gridlines in a table will incur a penalty only if these result in empty cells
	
	• Where lines of ruling have been inserted, a penalty under 4B will not be incurred for failure to leave a clear linespace below the column headings
	
	• Any consistent style of numbered paragraphs/items is acceptable eg 1.1) 1 or (1)

4M inconsistent use of open or full punctuation within a document	This includes: • A full stop appearing in any abbreviation such as *enc*, *cc*, *eg*, *am* when open has been used

	• A missing full stop in any abbreviation such as *enc.*, *c.c.*, *e.g.*, *a.m.* where full punctuation has been used
4N insertion of an additional comma which alters the meaning of a sentence	• Candidates should key in punctuation as dictated. However, the insertion of an additional comma will only be penalised if this alters the meaning of the sentence
4P failure to align text and figures in columns to the left, right or centre consistently - failure to align data in columns consistently with column headings	• Where sums of money require the alignment of decimal points in a column, the first figure should be left-aligned with the column heading
4Q failure to align decimal points within a document	

KNOWLEDGE, UNDERSTANDING AND SKILLS

3

This section provides explanatory notes and exercises for each of the types of documents similar to those you will have to complete in the exams. The notes and exercises for each different exam unit are grouped together.

The exercises are similar to the tasks you will have to complete in the exams, with circled instructions at the top of each document similar to those in the exam papers.

Notes pages

Notes pages precede each set of exercises. They explain how you should lay out documents and how to deal with the editing instructions. Take the time to read and understand the notes relating to each set of exercises before attempting them. You can refer to the notes as you work through each exercise.

Practice exercises

There are three new practice exercises for each type of document. Recall text for these exercises is available on the Hodder Plus website (see below). Once you have completed an exercise, proofread it and correct any errors. Save it using the filename indicated and print a copy. Find the correct worked example of the exercise in the 'Worked Examples' section on the Hodder Plus website and proofread your copy against this. If you are a member of a group, you may find it helpful to proofread each other's work.

Recall text from the Hodder Plus website

You will need to access files on the Hodder Plus website at **www.hodderplus.co.uk/ocrtextprocessing** to carry out the following:

- open and use templates for letter and fax
- recall text and amend as instructed
- access dictation for the audio-transcription exercises and practice exams
- access worked examples for all practice exercises and exams.

To access these files you will need to enter the following username and password:

username: text processing
password: recall1

The templates that you will need to recall are saved under the following file-names:

LETTERHEAD
FAX

For the purpose of these exercises and practice exams, you may use the same letterhead for any of the Text Production or Audio-Transcription documents, although some of the worked examples may show different letterheads. The same applies to the other templates, where slight variations may occur.

The text and graphics that you will need to recall for Word Processing are saved under the filenames given to you in each document in the practice exercises and exams.

Audio-Transcription

The Candidate Information Sheets (containing proper nouns) and Instruction to Invigilator Sheets (with information for document 3) are provided in this section. Dictated material is saved under filenames given to each exercise and accessed from the Hodder Plus website at **www.hodderplus.co.uk/ ocrtextprocessing**. In the exam you must use the recall material provided by OCR.

TEXT PRODUCTION LEVEL 3 PRACTICE EXERCISES

WITH DETAILED NOTES ON HOW TO WORK THE FOLLOWING DOCUMENTS:

- Letter
- Fax
- Minutes
- Terms of Reference
- Contract
- Report
- Article

LETTERS

Layout and style of a business letter

You will be required to produce a business letter in each of the Text Production and Audio-Transcription exams. For these exercises, a letterhead template will be provided on the Hodder Plus website. The font style, size and position of this must be retained. The body of the text may be in a different font, but must be easy to read. Arial 11 or Times New Roman 12 are popular.

Open punctuation is used in all OCR exams and in these exercises. This means that punctuation is inserted only where essential (eg full stops, apostrophes) or to clarify meaning (eg commas, brackets, dashes). Copy the punctuation given in the draft, but look out for missing full stops or misplaced/ missing/superfluous apostrophes in the Text Production letter.

The sample letter that follows is in blocked style (each line starting at the left margin), apart from the letterhead, and is in open punctuation. This is the style used in OCR exams. There must be at least one clear linespace between each separate item, with equal spacing between paragraphs.

Date

You must date each letter with the date on which you take the exam. No instruction will be given in the draft, but a reminder is given on the front cover of the question paper. A good position for the date is before or after the reference, although other positions are acceptable. The following styles are all acceptable:

10 August 2009   10th August 09   August 10 2009   10 Aug 09   10.8.09
10/08/09   10/08/2009

The example that is all in figures is more suitable for forms. In this style of date, if the month is shown before the day (ie 8.10.09), a penalty will be incurred, as it could be read as 8 October 2009.

Reference

Our ref must be displayed as shown in the draft. Follow the spacing, punctuation and capitalisation when keying in the actual reference. Do not add your initials to a reference as this will incur a penalty.

Special mark

In the Text Production and Audio-Transcription exams, you have to key in a special mark. This is used to show special treatment of the document (eg *By Hand, Urgent* or *Private and Confidential)*. If you place it immediately before the name and address of the recipient, it is less likely to be omitted when addressing an envelope or label, and it can be seen clearly through a window envelope. Follow the capitalisation given in the draft.

Name and address

Follow draft with regard to capitalisation. If the recipient's first name is drafted in full, that is how it should be keyed. Substituting an initial would be penalised.

Usual business practice is to show the name of the town in closed capitals, with the name of the county in initial capitals. In OCR exams and these exercises, abbreviations for *Drive, Street, Crescent*, and so on, should be expanded, but the county may remain abbreviated (see section 3.5 of the specification for a list of abbreviations for expansion). The postcode should be keyed with one space between its two parts. It may appear on a separate line, or on the same line as the town/county and separated from it by several spaces, as shown below:

Mr Sane Khor
Computer Courses
MANCHESTER   M5 2JT

Salutation and complimentary close

The salutation and complimentary close need to follow business practice. Do not mix the styles – *Dear Sir* should not be followed by *Yours sincerely*, but always by *Yours faithfully.* The styles should match, as shown below:

Dear Sir(s)/Madam … Yours faithfully
Dear Sane/Mr Khor … Yours sincerely

Leave at least four clear linespaces for the signature. If the letter runs into a second page, then at least two lines of text should be carried over to the continuation sheet, along with the complimentary close. You must also number the second page.

Subject heading

Key the subject heading, given in the instructions, after the salutation, as shown in the following sample business letter. Follow capitalisation given in the draft and leave a clear linespace before and after the heading.

Enclosure(s)

If the text indicates that an item/items are being enclosed, attached or included, you must show this at the end of the letter below the signatory details. Any appropriate methods are acceptable but you must show clearly whether there are single or multiple enclosures. For example:

Enc/Encs   enc/encs   ENC/ENCS   Att/Atts   ATT/ATTS

Copies and routing

In OCR Word Processing and Audio-Transcription exams and exercises you must provide two extra copies of the letter, showing the destination and routing on each copy. The most straightforward method is to key all the details at the bottom of the original copy and show the routing on copies 1 and 2, as follows:

Original	*1st copy*	*2nd copy*
Copy Eddie Lanteri	Copy Eddie Lanteri √	Copy Eddie Lanteri
File	File	File √

You may prefer to tick the copies manually using a pen (not pencil), or by high-lighting, emboldening or underlining. It is not essential for the details to appear on the original copy. This is called a *blind copy*, when these details appear only on the extra copies.

Continuation sheet

Where the letter goes on to a second page, that page should be printed on plain A4 paper. You should also number the second page if the letter runs on, but no other details need appear other than your candidate name and centre number.

Letterhead of Writer	**Progress Group** **Westwood Way** **COVENTRY** **CV4 8JQ** **024 7647 0033**
Date letter prepared	20 August 2009
Writer's reference	Our ref AC/jpd/L208
Receiver's reference	Your ref SK/098
Special mark	URGENT
Name and address of person to whom the letter is written	Mr Sane Khor Computer Courses MANCHESTER M5 2JT
Salutation	Dear Mr Khor
Subject heading	TEXTBOOK ORDER KME L208
Paragraphs of text	Thank you for your order for the sets of the revised edition of Keyboarding Made Easy, which will be available in bookshops next week.
	I have arranged for the copies to be dispatched to you by DPL. I trust this will meet your deadline. In the meantime, I am enclosing an advance copy, for your personal use.
	You mentioned in your email that you are starting a new business course. You may find our current catalogue of interest, a copy of which is also enclosed. There is an excellent range of packages covering subjects such as the internet, desktop publishing, databases and spreadsheets.
	Thank you for your custom and do not hesitate to contact us if we can be of further assistance.
Complimentary close	Yours sincerely
Space for signature of sender	
Name of sender	April Chaplin
Job title	Sales Executive
Enclosure(s) indicated	Encs
Person to receive copy	Copy Eddie Lanteri File

Amendments to text in letter document

Alterations to text

Refer to the 'Assessment Criteria' section of the Text Production Syllabus on page 11 for the list of amendment and correction signs. Some of these will appear in the following exercises.

Abbreviations and spellings

Abbreviations must be identified and expanded, and spelling errors identified and corrected. None of these will be circled at this level. The lists of abbreviations and spellings given in the 'Assessment Criteria' section of the Text Production Syllabus on page 11 contain the only words that will be tested in this way in this unit.

Apostrophe and punctuation errors

Any apostrophe errors must be identified and corrected. They may be superfluous, misplaced or missing, but will not be circled.

The punctuation error for you to correct will either be an omitted full stop or no capital following a full stop. The position will not be circled at this level.

Grammatical errors

The errors of agreement must be identified and corrected by you. They will not be circled and some will be less obvious at this level, eg *The reason we have made these rules are because there have been problems* or *The main office and the staff restaurant was damaged by fire.*

Incorporate information

There will be an instruction to find a multiple-word item in the Resource Sheet for you to key into the letter. The exact insertion point will be clearly indicated.

Postdating

There will be an instruction to provide a date for a precise day in the following month. Only the day and month need be inserted, as you do not need the year, eg *We look forward to seeing you on Friday 28 August.* The style used must be consistent throughout the document and should be the same style as the letter date.

EXERCISE TP 3.1

Letter to Mrs R Mason 76 Oak Ave COVENTRY CV3 4BH
Our ref PF/RJ Please use the heading HOME SHOPPING
CATALOGUE

Your ref CE/LN

Mark this PRIVATE

Dear Mrs Mason

Thank you for your recent order. Unfortunateley the items you require is not currently in stock. We are expecting a new delivery next week and immed we receive these items we will send them to you. // With ref to your question regarding direct debits we enclose a page giving you details of the companys sort code and account number. We are trying to encourage all of our customers to make payments by direct debit. We incur less expence when our customers use this method of payment. as soon as you start to pay using direct debit you will be eligible to receive a free gift. You may ~~select~~ ~~choose~~ your ✓ gift from the misc section in our catalogue. You will find items in this section that is suitable for the home and your choice of gift can be valued up to (please insert value here).

ready for next season

The new catalogue is being printed. You should receive your copy of this by Wednesday (give date for last Wednesday of next month).

There will be larger sections for kitchen equipment, clothes and shoes. If you place an order within two week of receipt you will be entitled to a discount and further info will be sent to you with the catalogue.

Yours sncly

for women, men and children

Paula Field
Sales Assistant

RESOURCE SHEET

DOCUMENT 1

Customers are able to select items valued up to a maximum of £25 when choosing a free gift.

EXERCISE TP 3.2

Letter to Mrs H Dickson 60 Downham Pl SALHOUSE Norfolk
NR13 4TP   Our Ref BW/kcr   Please use the heading
BREAKDOWN PROTECTION PLAN

Your Ref HD

Mark this PERSONAL

Dr Mrs Dickson

Thank you for choosing to buy one of our dishwashers. We can assure you that your appliance are of the highest quality. Your free gntee, *lasting for 12 months,* include labour, parts and call-out charges. [You now have the opp to register for a further year without any ~~further charges~~ ~~extra cost~~. You can do this by completing Part A of the enclosed form. At the end of this period, we recomend that you extend your cover with our Breakdown Protection Plan which will insure you for another (please add the additional length of time here). In the event of your dishwasher breaking down, the cost of all repairs are met. On request, an experienced engineer will mend the appliance asap free of charge. In addition, the bill will be settled directly with the repairer. This means that you will not have the hassle of completing any paperwork.

The cost of this insurance is £90 and will give you peace of mind for the next 5 year's. Any suitable method of payment is acceptable. to apply for this extra protection, please fill in Part B of the above-mentioned form which must be returned by Friday (give date for first Friday of next month).

We look forward to hearing from you very soon.

Yows sncly

You would even be covered for accidental damage.

Brian Woodstock
Customer Services Manager

RESOURCE SHEET

DOCUMENT 1

Your dishwasher comes with a free guarantee for one year and, in addition, you can register for another year's cover at no extra cost. After that, for a payment of £90, you will be insured for an additional 3 years. By completing Part B of the form, you will have peace of mind should your appliance break down during this time.

EXERCISE TP 3.3

Letter to Mrs Zoe Mansfield Wisteria Cottage Farmhouse Lane GROBY LE14 8BJ Our ref JDM/2014 Please use the heading ACCOUNT NUMBER 461398MA

Your ref ZM/BGA

Mark this PRIVATE AND CONFIDENTIAL

Dear Mrs Mansfield

I am pleased to advise you that your (add name here) bond will mature at the end of this month and your final balance of £7,865 will be available for re-investment. Despite the current low interest rates, we is delighted to offer you a highly competitive rate of 4.01% AER, guaranteed until your account matures again on 30 Nov 2011. This is a significant premium of 3.25% above the Bank of England Base Rate.

If you would like to reinvest/ *in the new bond*, they do not have to take any action. There are no complicated forms to complete. You do not have to sign any additional docs. Your account info and passbook will remain unchanged

If you would like to withdraw some funds from your account you may do so without charge during the penalty-free withdrawal period. You have until Friday (give date of last Friday of next month) to completes the transaction, but we recomend that you allow 7 working days' for your application to reach us.

(✓) If you have any ~~further questions~~ ~~more concerns~~, please do not hesitate to tel us direct on 024 7647 0033. A member of our Customer Service Team will be delighted to discus matters with you. Thank you for saving with Progress.

Alternatively, you could visit our website at www.progress-savings.co.uk

Yrs sncly

James David McGivern
Customer Service Manager

RESOURCE SHEET

DOCUMENT 1 – Letter

Progress Savings offer clients current and savings accounts. The company also operates a Progress Fastsave bond. Additionally, they offer more high-risk investments.

FAX/MINUTES/TERMS OF REFERENCE/CONTRACT

Layout and style

A template is provided for the fax on the Hodder Plus website at **www. hodderplus.co.uk/ocrtextprocessing**. Add the details shown in the draft against the relevant headings. Use the mouse or cursor keys to move between headings, to avoid creating extra linespaces. Do not add punctuation after the headings or infill details.

You do not need to recall templates for the other document types.

Date

The fax must be dated. No instructions will be given on the draft, but in a real OCR exam a reminder will be given on the front cover of the question paper. You must not date the minutes, terms of reference or contract; you will be penalised for this.

Amendments to text

Refer to the 'Assessment Criteria' section of the Text Production Syllabus on page 11 for the list of amendment and correction signs. Some of these will appear in these documents.

Emphasis

You will be instructed to emphasise a portion of text, such as a heading, sentence, line or paragraph. This is usually carried out by emboldening, using closed capitals or changing the font style/size. Make sure you emphasise only the section indicated.

Underline

A word in the main text of the document will be underlined. When keying the underline make sure that it does not extend to the spaces either side of the word.

Incorporate information

In this test, only the initial letter of one word will be drafted. You will need to find that word in the Resource Sheet so that you can complete the word in your document. It will be pretty obvious – for example, your draft may show C_____ *Kitchens* and the Resource Sheet will mention a firm called *Countrywide Kitchens*. You then complete the word *Countrywide* in your document.

Abbreviations and spellings

Abbreviations must be identified and expanded, and spelling errors identified and corrected. None of these will be circled at this level. The lists of abbreviations and spellings given in the 'Assessment Criteria' section of the Text Production Syllabus on pages 11–13 contain the only words that will be tested in this way in this unit.

Apostrophe error

You must identify and correct any apostrophe errors, which will not be circled at this level. Apostrophes will be either missing, misplaced or superfluous.

Numbered items

There will be a list containing numbered items. You will have to rearrange three of them according to the corrections shown in the draft.

Table

A two- to four-column table will be included in each of these documents. Although it is possible to use preset tabs or tabs that you have set yourself, it will be easier to manipulate text if you use the tables facility.

If you need a reminder about using the tables facility, refer to the Word Processing notes on tables in this section (pages 111–12).

There are several points you should bear in mind when keying the table in these documents.

- The spacing between each column does not have to be the same.
- There should be a clear linespace between headings and the first row of text.
- Ruling should not be shown in the printout of these types of document.

Attachment(s)

In the fax document, an attachment may be indicated. The same rules apply as those given for business letters.

EXERCISE TP 3.4

1 page fax from Angela Hobson to Anne Woodman at Praxi Ltd, ref AH/403 – fax number 020 8303 7699

CONTRACT AWARDS

SOUTHERN REGION

last Friday

Thank you for the talk on your co and how you would run this contract. My coleagues and I have given this award a great deal of thought. After much consideration we are happy to award to you this new contract for the coming year.

The contract is for:

LOCATION	VALUE £	PERSONNEL REQUIRED
Brighton	80,000	Manager and copy typist
Dover	50,000	Supervisor and three clerks
Margate	20,000	Senior Manager
Reading	12,000	Four word processor operators
Swindon	40,000	Junior Manager
Bath	10,000	Three audio typist's
Taunton	15,000	Senior Manager and assistant

The values represent the current ~~annual~~ yearly turnover. ✓

These sums are expected to _increase_ over the next year.

Outstanding matters are:

1 weekly sales targets
2 invoicing procedures
3 monthly a/cs
6 payment of salaries
4 temp staff
5 progress reports

for both of our businesses

Emphasise this sentence

Please contact my sec to arrange a time for the meeting on Tues.

As stated in the I_____ to Tender the contract ~~as set out~~ can be extended for a further twelve months.

I look forward to a successful contract next year.

Please acknowlege receipt of this fax.

RESOURCE SHEET

DOCUMENT 2

The Invitation to Tender stated that the contract can be extended for a peiod of one year.

EXERCISE TP 3.5

1 page fax from Emily Butcher to Henry Golding at Blackdown Recruitment, ref EB/vac4 – fax number 01666 057576

As promised on the phone last Thurs, I am giving below a list of our current job vacancies.

Personal Assistant	Marketing	Full-time
Filing Clerk	Human Resources	Temp
Project Leader	Construction	Full-time
Wages Clerk	Accounts	Part-time

I should be grateful if you would ~~send~~ ~~forward~~ names of suitable applicants with details of their qualifications and experience. All the jobs require good communication skills' and the ability to pay attention to detail. The successful person must be able to work well as a team member.

As we are anxious to fill these vacancies asap, interviews will be held at the end of this month.

Those shortlisted for interview should be prepared to submit the following info:

1 Contact details of two referees
~~2 Length of notice required by current employer~~
2 Earliest available starting date
5 Details of any h_____ already booked
3 Reasons for leaving present post (if applicable)
4 Evidence of good communication skills *for one or more of these posts*

If you have no suitable applicants Please fax me immed. We will then place an advertisment without delay in the local press. The full-time posts must be filled within the next six weeks.

Please emphasise this sentence

RESOURCE SHEET

DOCUMENT 2 – FAX

If selected for interview, your would-be employer will certainly want to know how soon you could start and if you have any holiday booked. You will no doubt be asked why you wish to leave your present employment.

EXERCISE TP 3.6

1 page fax from Simon Wallace to Melanie Grainger at Jephson International, ref SW/487 – fax number 01863 941837

✓ Following our ~~conversation~~ discussions about the appt of a Senior Administrator in your Accounts Dept, I am pleased to report that we have three candidates for interview. Their details are as follows:

FULL NAME	AREA	CURRENT SALARY
Harry Arthur	Logistics	£19,850
Jade Murphy	Accounts	£21,500
Stephen Jukes	Finance	£20,695

as soon as poss when and

I have spoken to all three candidates and they are very impressive. I will forward copies of their CVs ~~within the next couple of days~~. You will see that they have the new experiance to perform the role well.

Emphasise this sentence

Please let me know where you would like the formal meetings to take place.

In the meantime, I shall be advertising for the following staff (in the national press) to join your company:

1   Human Resources Assistant
3 2   Logistics Administrator
4 3   Mailroom Supervisor
2 4   Junior Receptionist

Please let me know by Fri next if you wish to make any changes. The advertissements will appear in the Weekly O____ within the next three week's. I will keep you informed of progress.

and person specifications
The job descriptions have already been prepared and I will forward a copy to you for confirmation.

RESOURCE SHEET

DOCUMENT 2 – Fax

The Weekly Observer is the preferred location for advertisements.

EXERCISE TP 3.7

MONTHLY DEPARTMENTAL MEETING

AT 10.30 AM

IN MEETING ROOM 3 ON SECOND FLOOR

The following people were present:

NAME	TITLE
Kate Willis (Chair)	Manager
Sarah Ali (minutes)	Supervisor
Mark Wong	Clerical Assistant
James Field	Audio Typist
Laura Steele	Secretary
Sue Ling	Office Junior
Edel Cole	Copy Typist

Emphasise this sentence

Apologies were recieved from Jo Barnes and Lhesley Carr.

The secretary ~~distributed~~ read the minutes of the last meeting. These were approved. The objectives had been attained for the preceding month in full. ✓

The Chair outlined the new objectives for the next four week's as follows:

1 review all job descriptions
2 amend the procedures doc
5 ~~3~~ undertake a complete stock check
3 ~~4~~ shred confidential waste paper
4 ~~5~~ change all computer passwords
6 schedule a fire practice drill asap

thanked staff for attending and

Using temp staff during busy periods to help out was discused.

It was agreed to employ one person to answer the tel and carry out clerical ~~and typing~~ duties.

It was announced that the contract for the supply of T——— Services had been renewed. This adds a further three yrs to this contract.

The Chair fixed the date for the next meeting. Finally at 11.30 am the meeting was closed.

RESOURCE SHEET

DOCUMENT 2

An announcement was made that the contract for Transcription Services had been renewed adding a further three years to the contract.

EXERCISE TP 3.8

Minutes of Progress Conservation Group Committee Meeting held on 13 Jan 2010 at 10 am in Room 5

PRESENT   Oliver Woods   Chair
                 Glenda Green   Sec
                 June Grainger   Treasurer
                 Peter Long
                 Leslie Lethbridge   *emphasise this heading*
                 Anna Tufail

APOLOGIES FOR ABSENCE were received from Gunther Weiss.

MINUTES OF THE LAST MEETING were read, confirmed and signed.

MATTERS ARISING   Peter Long asked if planning permission for developpment at southborough on the site of the old barns had been ~~granted~~ approved. Oliver Woods offered to make some enquiries and report back to the next meeting.

WEEKEND CONF ON GREEN ISSUES

The following planning list was drawn up:

1   Date
2   Venue
4 ~~3~~   Cost
5 ~~4~~   Speakers
3 ~~5~~   Title
6   Invitations

It was agreed that a s——— meeting was necy to plan this event. Glenda Green would email committee members' with suggested dates.

ANY OTHER BUSNESS   A letter had been received outlining plans for two wind turbines to be erected in the river valley. After much discussion, it was decided to oppose the application. Leslie Lethbridge offered to draft a reply to this effect for approval by the committee asap. ~~The draft would be sent by email.~~

DATE OF NEXT MEETING would be fixed after the special meeting.

from the County Planning Officer

RESOURCE SHEET

DOCUMENT 2 – MINUTES

The Progress Conservation Group committee decided to hold a special meeting to plan the weekend event on green issues. Glenda Green would suggest a few dates and email these to committee members.

EXERCISE TP 3.9

(Please emphasise this sentence)

MINUTES OF MEETING

A meeting of the Business Administration Team was held at 1600 hours in the IT Suite on Thur 14 June.

ATTENDANCE   NAME   POSITION

Judy Graham   Team Leader and Chair
Toni Malcolm   Tutor
Grace Needham   Tutor
Mark Andrews   Internal Verifier
Vikki Sturgess   Tutor

APOLOGIES FOR ABSENCE

There were no apologies for absence.

MINUTES OF LAST MEETING

and correct

The minutes of the previous meeting were accepted as a true/record of proceeding's. They were signed by the Chair.

COURSE INFORMATION SHEETS

Course information sheets, containing details of

1   course content
2³   assessment methods
3⁴   work experience opps   (for the Diploma in Administration)
4²   available options
5   progression routes

✓ had been prepared for all courses and were checked for ~~errors~~ accuracy. Judy thanked the team for their hard work at a busy time of year.

VERIFICATION VISIT

The External Verifier had arranged an appt for late June. Vikki confirmed that all student p——— were complete and a sample had been internally verified.

TIMETABLES

Judy reported that timetables for the next academic year were being prepared. If poss, staff would receeve a provisional copy by early July.

DATE OF NEXT MEETING

It was decided to hold a meeting in Sept. ~~The date was not agreed.~~

RESOURCE SHEET

DOCUMENT 2 – Minutes

The External Verifier will check student portfolios.

EXERCISE TP 3.10

TERMS OF REFERENCE

RELOCATION COMMITTEE

The ~~group~~ committee is authorised to procure quotes for the new ✓ building in North Rd. The services required are:

SERVICE	BUDGET £
Rubbish and recycling collection	5000
Boxes or crates for packing	2000
Removal vans and staff	8000
Security system for door's and lifts	5000
Updating kitchen facilities	6000

There must be a minimum of one person from each dept on the committee.

The committee will hold a mtg once a week until the move takes place.

Other items for disscussion are:

1 off-site storage facilities for old docs
2 new internal tel system
4 the basement storage area
5 new desks and chairs
3 removal of computers and other electrical equipment
6 acess to the internet during the move

A total budget of £ ____ has been allocated for the move.

Emphasise this sentence

The move to take place over two days in order to ensure that the company can continue to conduct business.

The committee to appoint a chairman who will write a report each week. detailing the progress to date

Staff ~~and the committee~~ will be told when the new lease has been signed.

Everyone to ensure that business continues as usual while preparations for the move take place.

RESOURCE SHEET

DOCUMENT 2

To cover the cost of the move the company has allocated a total budget of £150,000 for all the expenses incurred by the relocation of the offices.

EXERCISE TP 3.11

PROGRESS CONSERVATION GROUP

At its committee mtg last month, Progress Conservation Group expressed its grave concern for a large housing complex to be built close to a local beauty spot.

As a result, it was agreed to set up a seperate group to look specifically into the effects on the environment of this new project. Approx 700 homes are to be built near an area of outstanding beauty and on the ~~outskirts~~ edge of an ✓ award-winning N_____ village.

over the newly published proposals

The groups' objectives will be to

1	liaise with the city and county planning depts
2	obtain a _detailed_ map of the site
3	look into the effects on the local infrastructure
6 ~~4~~	consider other sites for the project
4 ~~5~~	consult experts on the poss harm to wildlife
5 ~~6~~	put forward ideas on green issues
~~7~~	~~submit new proposals by the required date~~
7	meet the set deadline for reccomendations

The committee will comprise

Janine Anguish	Chair	Progress Conservation
Angus McMahon	Sec	Green Spaces
Azine Mahmoud	Treasurer	Progress Conservation
John Adelhaid		Environmental Officer
Nicola Woodside		County Planner

The group will be set up for six months initially.
Any objections to the development must be submitted in writing to the County Planning Officer within this period.

emphasise this sentence

RESOURCE SHEET

DOCUMENT 2 – TERMS OF REFERENCE

Progress Conservation Group committee members are very concerned to hear of the proposal to build 700 new homes close to an award-winning village in Norfolk. The development site is very near to a beautiful river valley with its wildlife and nature trails.

EXERCISE TP 3.12

TERMS OF REFERENCE

PROGRESS EMPLOYEE SUPPORT GROUP

The above-named group will serve to support *and advise* members of staff who work for Progress International in any role. This group will provide guidance, advice and feedback to any employee who is in dispute with the co for reasons of accident or illness, pay award disagreements or matters relating to redundancy.

The group shall

2. provide a forum for ideas and discussions
3. make recommendations
1. act as a consultative comittee for work on these ~~matters~~ *issues* ✓
4. provide representation to m_____ in support of the employee

Please emphasise this sentence

The group will comprise representatives from all specialism's within the org.

Agreed procedures are as follows:

ITEM	AGREED PROCEDURE
Elections	To take place in Dec each yr
Number of members	No more than 15 members, representing all depts
Length of tenure	Members are appointed for a 12-month period

Meetings will be held monthly during working hours. The meetings will be conducted according to normal meeting procedures.

The group will ~~at all times~~ attempt to act through <u>consensus</u> decision-making. If a decision cannot be reached throgh this process, then a two-thirds majority will decide the issue.

Decisions will be recorded by the Chair.

led by the elected Chair and

RESOURCE SHEET

DOCUMENT 2 – Terms of Reference

The support group's role includes the provision of representation to management.

REPORT/ARTICLE

Layout and style

This document should be printed on plain A4 paper and has been designed to run on to several pages. It is not essential to number the first page, but numbering must appear on the continuation sheets. To customise your page numbering, use **Insert ➤ Page Numbers**.

Linespacing

Linespacing before and after headings and between paragraphs must be consistent within a document. You will be instructed to change the linespacing of several paragraphs of text.

Headings

Follow the draft regarding capitalisation of headings. Leave at least one clear linespace before and after headings consistently. A heading should not be on a different page to the start of its related paragraph.

Amendments to text

Refer to the 'Assessment Criteria' section of the Text Production Syllabus on page 11 for the list of amendment and correction signs. Some of these will appear in this document.

Footnotes

You are instructed to insert two footnotes in the report or article. Footnotes must always appear on the same page as the symbol[1] in the relevant text. Do not leave a space between the word and symbol in the text, but one space should be left after the symbol and the note that you key into the footnote pane at the bottom of the page (see below). Follow draft regarding punctuation in the note.

Make sure you are working in *Print Layout View*. Use **Insert ➤ Footnote and Endnote ➤** select **Footnote** and **AutoNumber ➤ OK**. A footnote pane will open at the end of your page for you to key in your footnote text. When you have finished just return your cursor to the main text to continue. If required, you can add more than one footnote to the same page by simply repeating these steps. (Note that different versions of software may have different methods for inserting footnotes. Refer to the help section of your package for further details on how to do this.)

[1] The symbol may be customised as *, ** or a, b, or any other relevant symbol, as you wish.

Abbreviations and spellings

Abbreviations must be identified and expanded, and spelling errors identified and corrected. None of these will be circled at this level. The lists of abbreviations and spellings given in the 'Assessment Criteria' section of the Text Production Syllabus on pages 11–13 contain the only words that will be tested in this way in this unit.

Typographical errors

These are words containing extra, omitted or transposed letters and extraneous symbols. They are not circled at this level, but must be identified and corrected.

Apostrophe and punctuation errors

There will be either missing, misplaced or superfluous apostrophes. You must identify these and correct them.

There will be either omitted full stops at the end of sentences or no initial capital following a full stop. You must identify these and correct them.

Inset text

You will be instructed to inset a section of text from the left margin. The measurement must be exact. To ensure this, select the text, then use **Format ➤ Paragraph ➤ Indents and Spacing ➤** select **Indentation Left ➤** and key in the correct measurement.

Centre

You will be instructed to centre a line or section of text. Select the text to be centred then click on the **Align Center** icon. Make sure you return to left align after that section.

Underline

In the draft, several words in the body of the text will be underlined. You should follow the draft, making sure that the underlining does not extend beyond the first and last words of that section. You can ensure this by highlighting the section carefully and clicking the underline icon.

Incorporate information

The Resource Sheet contains four items of information, two of which you will need to incorporate into this document. There will be a single-word item and a multiple-word item.

EXERCISE TP 3.13

Use double linespacing except where indicated

CRUISING WITH PROGRESS GROUP LINERS *centre this heading*

THE PROGRESS QUEEN OF ADVENTURE

A new addition to our fleet is due to sail on its maiden voyage in Feb next year. The new boat is being fitted to a high standard and will give passengers a holiday to remember for the rest of their lives

The Progress Queen of Adventure is not as large as the other liners in our fleet. This is to allow the boat to dock in smaller ports that are inaccessible to the larger liners. We have ~~very frequently~~ been asked if we can sail into some of the smaller and more interesting ports on our cruises. Now we can dock and our passengers can explore many of the old and quaint towns along the route.

The maiden voyage will be for ten days and will include some lovely Mediterranean ports[1] where passengers can disembark.

_____

[1] our brochure gives a detailed list

EXCURSIONS

(these paragraphs only in single linespacing)

Optional excursions are available ~~There will be a wide variety of interesting trips offered to passengers~~ at all ports. Passengers can either join an organised trip or explore on their own. // The length of time the boat will stay in dock varies but will be approx ten hours. This allows time for coach trip's and some very exciting excursions have been planned.

Our aim is to give passengers the opp to see sights that are off the main tourist routes. We think this offers the best way to experiense the historic regions.

ENTERTAINMENT

The Progress Queen of Adventure has been built with three lounges. Each evening the entertainment will be in the main lounge ~~Every night we will have singers, musicians and comedians to entertain you~~.

There will be many singers and musicians who will provide a range of music to suit most tastes. For example, one evening may be jazz music and the next evening may be a clasical music night. A full programme of events will be given to passengers when they embark. The two smaller lounges have large windows and these can be used by passengers who want to sit, relax and enjoy the views.

(close to the Mediterronean Sea)

DINING ON BOARD

Buffets are available for braekfast and lunch, but dinner is served at your table by waiting staff. The buffets offer an excellent variety of foods with somthing to suit everyone. A four-course dinner is served each evening and diners have six choices for each course. The boat will take on fresh fruit and vegetables at each port and where poss we buy local produce. We are also able to buy a selection of fresh seafood from the local ____.

ACTIVITIES ON BOARD

Passengers can enjoy using the spa complex and swimming pool which is on the top deck. There is a fitness room and exercise classes willl be held at regular times during the day.

The hairdressing salon will be run by Karen White who has been a hairdresser for many years and has won ~~several prestigious~~ awards for her styles and products. Next to the hairdressing salon will be a beauty parlour where treatments such as ____ ____ ____ can be booked.

There will be several days when the boa6t is at sea and will not sail into any ports. We have a full schedule of activities beginning after breakfast. There will be films shown through out the day in the cinema and an excellent programme of games, classes and demonstrations is planned.

BOOKINGS

inset this paragraph 25 mm from left margin

We are offering discounts of up to fifty per cent[2] if you can book the cruise before the end of this year. Prices will vary depending on the type of cabin you select. The staff working in our booking office are able to help you choose exactly the right cabin to meeet your requirements. PLease contact Progress Gruop Liners for more information and we will be happy to send you a brochure.

We have other vessels that sail all over the world and if you enjoy cruising holidays you will find our brochure very interesting. We beleive you will have a wonderful holiday with Progress.

[2] on selected cabins only

RESOURCE SHEET

DOCUMENT 3

The buffets offer a wide variety of foods with something to suit all tastes. There are buffets for breakfast and lunch with four-course dinners in the evening.

Passengers can book treatments such as facials and manicures in the beauty parlour which is situated next to the hairdressing salon.

At some ports we are able to buy locally grown fruit and vegetables. A good selection of fresh seafood from the local fishermen can also be purchased.

The maiden voyage will be for ten days and will include many Mediterranean ports where passengers can disembark.

EXERCISE TP 3.14

Double linespacing except where indicated

LIFELONG LEARNING ← *centre this heading*

Learning continues throughout life and in many diffferent situations. It does not stop when we leave school. So often we hear people say "I've learnt something new today," or "well, I never knew that before". Lifelong learning is well provided for, as outlined below.

EVENING CLASSES

Traditionally, adult education has been thought of as attending an evening class. Over the years many different subjects have been taught, from leisure pursuits and hobbies *, to more serious academic subjects* that can lead to a recogn9ised qualification. In the past our evening classes have been well thought of throughout the world.

However, a few years ago, in order to concentrate on improving employment skills, a level of funding was withdrawn from vocational courses such as pottery, bridge and flower arranging. This resulted in a huge drop in adult attendance because the cost was too high. Many classes were forced to close as minimum numbers were not met.

In an attempt to reverse the downward trend in attendance, a new initiative has been put forward. This aims at persuading vacant high street shops, churches, museums, libraries, ~~or galleries and public houses~~ etc to open up rooms at a modest charge. The idea is to encourage people to organise their own evening classes. *A limited amount* ~~Internet facilities in~~ *of financial help would be available for such schemes.* ~~libraries, for example, are used by many people to further their knowledge~~ A number of orgs ~~and local authorities~~ have already backed this initiative.

these paragraphs only in single linespacing

IMPROVING EMPLOYMENT SKILLS

For those wishing to boost their employment prospects or further their career, there are many options. Study can be part time, full time, over a few weeks or just a few hours. A degree course of three or more years is another poss alternative.

There is the choice between enrolling at a local college or studying at home. You should be certain of good tuition and one-to-one support whatever you decide to do.

Home study, or distance learning, requires a considerable amount of sellf-discipline and the ability to meet deadline's. The flexibility offered allows study to fit in with work and family commitments. Achieving set goals can be extremely rewarding. Gaining a qualification could lead to increased job security, a higher salary and an interesting career.

There are ———— of courses on offer. Many of these do not require any entry qualifications. Therefor, if you left school with very little to show but are now motvated to learn some thing new, there will certainly be a course to suit you. You could start by searching online. on the other hand, you may prefer to talk to someone face to face. In this case, your local careers office should be your first step.

A few examples of continuing education availalbe to school leavers and adults of all ages are given below.

VOCATIONAL COURSES

These focus on doing things and learning practical skills such as hairdressing, plumbing* and office

* qualified plumbers are always needed

work. A period of training in the workplace is necy. Certificates and diplomas are awarded by a number of different examination boards. Vocational study can be undertaken (at colleges of further education (and) at secondary schools).

DEGREE COURSES

For those who were not high achievers at school, or those who wish to improve their
grades, GCSEs may be studied or retaken at college/or by distance learning. , at evening classes

Job seeking courses **offer advice on how to write a curriculum vitae, on interveiw techniques and how to sell your strengths.

GCSEs

inset this paragraph 30mm from left margin

The Open University offers undergraduate and postgraduate courses. THese are modular in structure and can be combined over a length of time to lead to a degree. The _____ __ _____ course is recomended for those not familiar with higher education. [Distance learning for a degree, like the Open University, gives students freedom to work from home whenever time permits. There are also learning advisers to point you in the right direction. A personal tutor is there for guidance and help throughout.

Further info on all courses may be obtained from careers offices, job centres and online.

** go online for the nearest course

RESOURCE SHEET

DOCUMENT 3

Lifelong learning is well provided for. Evening classes and colleges of further education offer opportunities for study either full or part time during the day and evening. If you would prefer to study from the comfort of your own home, distance and home study courses are available. There are thousands of courses to choose from, some of which do not require any formal entry qualifications. The Open University is an option for those wishing to study for a degree. Students who have not previously studied to a higher level or who have not studied for many years should consider enrolling on the Preparing for Study course.

EXERCISE TP 3.15

double linespacing except where indicated

PROGRESS AUCTIONS

ASK THE EXPRETS!

Centre these headings

Progress Auctions is one of the United Kingdom's largest auction houses. We have more than 75 yrs' experrience of selling antiques and collectables to dealers and private buyers.

Our head office is in _____ but we now operate from ten regional salerooms. Each regional saleroom organises its own monthly auction and other specialist sales.

GENERAL AUCTIONS

Althogh many of us understand how an auction works, the finer detail is often less well-known. If you are not entirely sure of correct procedure, please ask a member of our team. They will be happy to advise you on how to prepare your goods for auction and the costs involved in buying at auction. This service Is completely free of charge.

FREE ADVICE AND GUIDANCE

Each month, all our regional salerooms put on a general sale. Categories include clocks, furniture, jewellery, paintings and other household items. The value of goods offered at a general auction may not be high and it is poss to purchase quality pieces at low prices. Check our website at www.progress-auctions.co.uk for details of the next general auction at your nearest saleroom.

SPECIALIST AUCTIONS

well in advance of the auction date

Specialist auctions are also held on a regular basis. Each sale attracts respected buyers and dealers from around the world and bids can reach six-figure sums. If you have an article which you wish to include in a specialist sale, please contact a member of our team. It would be helpful if any item to be sold had a certificate of provenance* to accompany it

*   indicating source of origin

These paragraphs only in single linespacing

BIDDING FOR ITEMS

It is always exciting to take part in the bidding process ~~Placing a bid on a desired article is great fun~~, but it makes sense to research the value of the item ****** before placing your bid.   Remember, too, that a buyers premium of approx 12.5% plus tax is payable on the hammer price. So what appeared to be a bargain may not, after payment of all charges,   turn out to be such a good deal!

Inset this paragraph 40 mm from left margin

If you are unable to be present but wish to bid for an item, our commission clerks will under take written and pos8tal bids on your behalf. Sale results are issued within 48 hours of the sale and items purchased must be removed from our auction roooms within 3 working days.

SELLING ITEMS

If you want to sell something, but do not want the price to fall below a certain amount, we can negotiate a fixed reserve price. If biding fails to reach the specified figure, we will not surrender the item.

We will charge a — — — — on sales of all items under £1,000 in value. Articles which exceed this value will be charged at a higher rate.

TRANSPORTATION AND STORAGE

Whether you are preparing an item for sale or taking your new purchase home, ~~Transportation of goods to and from the auction houses is a role where~~ the Progress team can help.

EAch of our regional offices has its own team of removal staff and a fleet of removal vans. For a small charge, we will be happy to move your goods. The fee includes insurance cover.

** Check the condition of the item carefully

FREE VALAUTIONS

If you are unsure of the value of an item, why not bring it in to your local Progress saleroom and let us assess its value? We can advise on insurance or *,if you wish,* give you *info about the next appropriate auction.*

If the item in queston is large, we can visit your home and give an on-site valuation of the piece. Our valuation experts organise visits all around the country and can advise on the value of the item and the best outlet for its sale. Please contact your local saleroom for details of this service.

We hope that you will decide to do business with Progress Auctions. We are sure you will find that the service we offer is second to none. We look forward to hearing from you soon, whether you are buying or selling!

RESOURCE SHEET

DOCUMENT 3 – Article

The United Kingdom has more than 50 registered auction houses.

The company's head office has recently moved to Coventry.

A vendor's commission of 15% is charged on all sales.

A buyer's premium amounts to approximately 12.5% plus tax.

WORD PROCESSING LEVEL 3 PRACTICE EXERCISES

WITH DETAILED NOTES ON HOW TO WORK THE FOLLOWING DOCUMENTS:

- Report
- Article
- Two Column Article
- Two Column Information Sheet
- Table
- Booklet
- Programme
- Leaflet

REPORT/ARTICLE

Margins and justification

You will be instructed to change the line length of this document. Deduct the specified line length from the width of the page (A4 = 21cm wide), divide the answer by two for equal left and right margins. Use **File ➤ Page Setup** to select the margins. Make sure that *Apply to Whole Document* is flagged. Highlight the text using **Control + A** and click the **Justify** icon.

Header and footer

You will be instructed to insert a header and footer in this document. Use **View ➤ Header and Footer** and use the icon to move from one to the other. Key in the text, using the font style and size specified, and use the alignment icon to place it correctly.

Amendments to text

Refer to the 'Assessment Criteria' section of the Word Processing Syllabus on page 24 for the list of amendment and correction signs. Some of these will appear in this document.

Inset text

When insetting a portion of text it is important that the measurement is exact.

To inset from the left and right margins, highlight the relevant text and use **Format ➤ Paragraph**, using the arrows in the left and right margin boxes to increase the paragraph indent.

Move and copy text

These are two distinct instructions and it is important that you understand the difference.

To **Move** a section of text use the **Cut** and **Paste** icons (or keyboard short-cuts **Ctrl + X** and **Ctrl + V**). The portion of text should appear only once in the document.

To **Copy** a section of text use the **Copy** and **Paste** icons (or keyboard shortcut **Ctrl + C** to copy). The portion of text should then appear twice in the document. For these exercises you need to copy a section twice, so that it appears three times in the document.

Vertical transposition

When transposing items vertically, be careful to switch the position of the circled words only, eg if only the paragraph headings are circled, the headings should be switched, but the paragraphs left in their original order. Be careful not to omit or move any intervening text.

Find and replace

You will be required to change between three and five instances of a recurring specified word in the document. Once all the text has been keyed, use **Edit →** **Replace** (or keyboard shortcut **Ctrl + H**), complete the **Find What** and the **Replace With** boxes with the appropriate words, and click **Replace All**. It is important to follow capitalisation and use the **Match case** option.

Sort list

Highlight the list and use **Table → Sort → Ascending**.

Change case

Highlight the section of text to be changed and use **Format → Change Case → select specified case** (or use keyboard shortcut **Shift + F3**).

Text box

To insert a text box use **Insert → Text Box** and drag it to the required size. To make the text wrap round all sides of the box, right click the box and select **Format Text Box → select Layout → select Square**. Click on *Centre* in the *horizontal alignment* section of the **Format Text Box** window to place the text box centrally within the paragraph.

Linespacing

You will be instructed to alter the linespacing of the recall text, except for one section of text. You can leave the linespacing alterations until you have completed the other editing instructions.

Page breaks and numbering

This can be left to the end of the exercise. To insert page breaks, position your cursor where you wish to start a new page and use **Control + Enter**. This formatting can be deleted by using the Show/Hide icon (¶) to reveal the page break instruction, highlighting *page break* and pressing **Delete**.

To insert page numbers, using **Insert** ➤ **Page Numbers** will let you fully customise your numbering. **View** ➤ **Header and Footer** can also be used.

EXERCISE WP 3.1

Recall the article stored as RENTAL and amend as shown. Adjust left and right margins to produce a line length of 13.5 cm. Change to double linespacing (except where indicated) and use full justification. Delete existing page breaks and insert new page breaks as appropriate. Number the pages starting with page 9. Print one copy.

ISSUES FOR THOUGHT

Having taken the decision to rent your holiday home, there are many issues which will need your careful thought.

Will you be able to recoup any ~~initial~~ outlay for furnishings or accessories, in order to make your property suitable for rental purposes?

which you may find helpful

Here are just a few issues. You will think of many more as you become more experienced.

or even for the cost of repairs,

Smoking/non-smoking
Electricity charges
General house hold appliances
Health and safety compliance
Kitchen appliances
Pets
Wood burner/central heating
Supplies of bed linen and towels
Suitable parking
Welcome pack

Sort into exact alphabetical order

Copy to Points marked ✸

If you want to turn this venture into a success, you will need to stand out from the rest to ensure guests have a memorable holiday. In this way they will want to return or recommend you to friends.

TARGET MARKET

Inset this section 2.5 cm from both left and right margins

about the type of holidaymaker

You need to think carefully ~~when deciding on client groups~~ for whom you are catering. [When furnishing your home, remember there will be significant wear and tear which will need replacement ~~or repair~~ at the end of each season. This needs to be taken into account when setting your rental prices.

Move to point ●

Think about whether you do or do not want families with children and pets, or will couples cause fewer problems?

✸

Change all occurrences of THOUGHT to CONSIDERATION throughout this document matching case as draft

Move to point marked ■

Keep a visitors' book. Recommendations by other holidaymakers are usually honest and unbiased. Offer headings such as best restaurant, most enjoyable local attraction, best walks.

(INFORMATION)

~~location~~

Thought needs to be given to the ~~situation~~ of your property. ✓ If you are near a beach, think of the sand which could be brought into your house. Are carpets the best floor covering? Maybe a tiled floor would be more suitable. Rugs can add warmth in the winter. When decorating, neutral colours generally appeal more to people. Brighter colours can be used for furniture and accessories. Walls are better painted, rather than wallpapered. It is much quicker to freshen a room with a coat of paint.

Insert a text box with border 6 cm wide by 3 cm high with the word ACCESSORIES. Ensure text box is centred horizontally within the paragraph and that text wraps around the text box on all sides

•

Ensure you are able to lock away all your valuable possessions that you do not want your guests to use.

(FURNISHINGS)

Think about what you personally like to find on holiday. What may seem trivial can actually be quite important. For example, prepare a list of local emergency contact details. Some tourist information centres provide a calendar advertising local events.

■

from talking to friends that

It can be very frustrating to return home only to discover / you missed a famous festival or carnival.

Change this sentence to upper case

✱ FINANCIAL AND LEGAL THOUGHTS

This paragraph only in single linespacing

Before you let your property, make sure in every aspect you comply with all the necessary legal requirements.

Choose a solicitor who is familiar with local authority regulations. You will need liability insurance in case guests injure themselves whilst at your property.

Insert HOLIDAY HOMES as a header in the centre and 4TH EDITION as a footer at the right margin. Use Comic Sans MS 8 font for the header and footer. Header and footer to appear on every page.

EXERCISE WP 3.2

Recall the article stored as INSURANCE and amend as shown. Adjust left and right margins to produce a line length of 12 cm. Change to double linespacing (except where indicated) and use full justification. Delete existing page breaks and insert new page breaks as appropriate. Number the pages starting with page 15. Print one copy.

PROGRESS GROUP INSURANCE DIVISION

(Y)

with years of expertise

We are a world-renowned company in the following areas:

Sort into exact alphabetical order

Credit and Store Card Protection
Home Contents
Medical and Health
Caravan and Mobile Home
Mortgage Protection
House and Buildings
Motorbike, Car and Van
Annual and Single-Trip Travel

Insert INSURANCE as a header at the left margin and PUBLICATION as a footer at the right margin. Use Arial font point size 10 for the header and footer. Header and footer to appear on every page

Move to point marked (Y)

This division of the Progress Group is able to provide all its Customers with an extensive range of tailor-made policies.

have travel, home and car

The majority of people ~~need many different types of~~ insurance. Below is a summary of these three categories.

MOTORING

Insert a text box with border 4 cm wide x 4.5 cm high with the word VEHICLES. Ensure the text box is centred horizontally within the paragraph and that the text wraps around the box on all sides.

Over 700,000 people have their car insurance with us. When your policy is next due for renewal we will give you a very competitive quote. Whether you drive a car, motorbike or van we are sure we will be able to offer you the same cover at a better price.

We will assign to you a personal claims manager if you have to make a claim. This means that each time you contact us you will speak to the same person until your claim has been satisfactorily resolved and your vehicle has been repaired.

copy to points marked (X)

In order to find out how much you could save by changing to Progress, please call us on 024 7647 0033.

Change all occurrences of customers to clients throughout this document matching case as draft

TRAVELLING

We pay for additional ~~hotel~~ accommodation when flights are delayed for more than twenty hours.

(Change this sentence to upper case)

Whether you travel for business purposes or for pleasure we know we can meet your requirements.

~~travel~~

Our ~~holiday~~ insurance includes cover for damaged, lost or stolen luggage. ✓

✗

YOUR HOME

Ⓩ

(up to a maximum of)

valued at more than

We can also provide cover if a single item is /£10,000. In order to do this we would need an independent valuation from an assessor.

(this paragraph only in single linespacing)

Our mortgage protection policies give all CUSTOMERS peace of mind. It is good to know that your mortgage payments will be made if you are unable to work. The reason you are not working is immaterial. It could be because of redundancy or ill-health. Mortgage protection will pay your mortgage for two years.

(Move to point marked Ⓩ)

If you combine your building and contents cover into one policy you will be entitled to a discount of ten per cent.

✗

FAMILY PETS

(Inset this section 1 cm from both left and right margins)

In response to many requests from existing customers we have decided to add pet cover onto our list of policies.//Without insurance cover ~~veterinary~~ bills can be very expensive. If you take your pet to a vet you could be faced with some high costs.

Premiums for pet insurance will vary depending on the kind of animal.

Customers will be able to include multiple pets on one policy.

With one of our policies you can make a claim each time you visit the vet.

Pet insurance is not available at the present time.

We will be able to provide this with effect from January next year.

EXERCISE WP 3.3

Recall the report stored as NEWS and amend as shown. Adjust left and right margins to produce a line length of 10cm. Change to double linespacing (except where indicated) and use full justification. Delete existing page breaks and insert new page breaks as appropriate. Number the pages starting with page 11. Print one copy.

PROGRESS LOCAL NEWS

Our aims and objectives are to

Change all occurrences of holidays to breaks throughout this document matching case as draft

offer deals
beat the competition
be innovative
consolidate readership
encourage participation
engage interest
introduce new ideas
increase revenue

Sort into exact alphabetical order

and direct year-on-year comparisons
The analysis of monthly figures/has been essential to focus attention on areas that are underperforming.

FEATURES SECTION

Interviews with local dignitaries and business people appear to have been well received. There is no shortage of candidates willing to take part in this series. The executive editor has received positive feedback from a large number of readers.

SHORT HOLIDAYS
Having successfully negotiated with a local coach firm
~~After putting our requirements out to tender~~, plans have been finalised to organise guided tours across the country. Holidays of 3-5 nights will be offered throughout the year. Accommodation will be in graded hotels and will include full board. [The holidays will have a theme. The first one is visiting stately homes and gardens in Somerset ~~and Dorset~~. We have secured the services of a tour guide.

Uptake of places has been brisk and these short holidays will provide substantial revenue.◄——— *Change this sentence to uppercase*

Insert LOCAL PRESS as a header at the left margin and FUTURE STRATEGY as a footer at the right margin. Use Times New Roman 9 font for the header and footer. Header and footer to appear on every page.

or a half-page advertisement for the price of a quarter-page

ADVERTISING

This is a ~~very~~ difficult area at the present time. Display advertising is down 20% compared with the same period last year. Special offers, including three insertions for the price of two, have boosted interest but many companies are cutting down on their regular advertising.

This section only in single linespacing

Recruitment advertising has halved. This sector of the market used to account for a high proportion of our display business. However, it remains depressed.

Action points need to be drawn up for ~~discussion~~ *consideration* at the next meeting.

COMMENTS AND OPINIONS

centred on the editor's column

The introduction of a discussion forum has caught our readers' imagination. They have contributed enthusiastically. It would appear that its success has been reflected in the recent increase in readership. This needs to be monitored carefully but for the moment participation shows no sign of abating.

Insert a text box with border 3.5 cm wide x 2.5 cm high with the word Debates Ensure text box is centred horizontally within the paragraph and that text wraps around the text box on all sides

Move to point marked ■

The regular meetings of subeditors have proved to be of enormous benefit in driving our group forward in a testing financial climate.

CONCLUSION

Inset this paragraph 2 cm from both left and right margins

Crosswords and number puzzles have been supplemented with quizzes, anagrams and mental arithmetic tasks. Market research indicates that this section appeals to all age groups. The introduction of a regular monthly two-page spread of various puzzles has been popular with everyone.

MENTAL EXERCISES

Classified advertising has seen a small rise in revenue but not enough to compensate for the downturn in overall advertising.

Move to point marked ◉

We have negotiated with local supermarkets for our publication to be placed for the next four weeks near the check-out tills. This provides us with an advantage over our competitors.

Our success will only continue by providing our readers with interesting and varied features and value for money.

Copy to points marked

ARTICLE/INFORMATION SHEET

Layout

This document is designed for displaying in two columns. Use *Print Layout View*, otherwise columns are displayed underneath each other and not side by side.

Track changes

Before keying or making any amendments, turn on track changes using **Tools** ➤ **Track Changes** ➤ **Highlight Changes** ➤ make sure **Track changes while editing**, **Highlight changes on screen** and **Highlight changes in printed document** are ticked and click **OK**.

You have to print one copy of the finished document showing the track changes and one without them. To remove the track changes, go back into **Highlight Changes** and cancel the ticks from all three boxes, click **OK**.

Note some packages have different options. Refer to the help pages of your package for further information.

Formatting text

Complete keying in and editing before formatting text into columns, except for inserting spacing, which should be done afterwards. Note that the column lengths will not necessarily be equal, but this is acceptable for the exam.

To format columns, select the text then use **Format** ➤ **Columns** ➤ select the number of columns required and key in the width.

EXERCISE WP 3.4

> Recall the information sheet stored as LETTING and amend as shown ensuring that track changes are displayed. Display the whole document in 2 columns (newspaper style) each column 5.5 cm wide. Do not change font style or size and retain full justification.

FREE GUIDE ON HOLIDAY LETTING

> Your earning potential will depend on several factors.

> Thinking of buying for investment or are you interested in generating an income from your current holiday home? Then read on.

You could try managing your holiday letting yourself, but most people do not find it as straightforward as they might at first think.

First and foremost is the location. ↗ A cottage /overlooking the sea, but within a reasonable distance of amenities and attractions, is more popular than an apartment in the middle of a village.
set on a headland

> and unfortunately the only thing beyond our control

Freedom, peace and a safe environment for the children provide all that is needed for the perfect family holiday – weather permitting.

> This does depend on the type of holiday required.

A suitably furnished cottage is important
~~The quality of the property attracts holidaymakers~~ as well as the number of people it can accommodate. Biggest is not always best.

> Keeping your holiday home in good repair is essential. [The ~~usual facilities~~ must be available, ✓ such as a washing machine, ~~microwave oven,~~ television etc, but if you want an advantage over your competitors you need to offer more, such as internet access, or indoor and outdoor games for the children.
~~normal appliances~~

We are experienced in property letting. Our shrewd marketing ensures the highest occupancy and maximum income. You tell us the number of weeks you want for your own use and leave the rest to us.

> Refer to the Resource Sheet and insert the paragraph on arranging a free, no obligation visit here

> Print one copy displaying the track changes. Accept all changes and print a second copy which does not show the track changes

RESOURCE SHEET

Arrange a free, no obligation visit to your holiday home and we will estimate your earning potential. This will be based on location and additional facilities that you can offer.

We have hundreds of satisfied owners who have used our business knowledge and advertising skills year after year. We are proud of our reputation. You have nothing to lose.

EXERCISE WP 3.5

Recall the information sheet stored as PARKS and amend as shown ensuring that track changes are displayed. Display the whole document in 2 columns (newspaper style), each column 5.5 cm wide. Do not change font style or size and retain full justification.

PROGRESS CARAVAN PARKS

We have ten parks throughout the UK and these are situated in lovely coastal locations. Whether for a weekend ~~away~~ or for a longer vacation our parks offer everything that is required for an enjoyable break.

Owning your own holiday caravan is a pleasure.

the exclusive use of

All our parks have separate bars and restaurants for owners. —

This provides the opportunity to meet other people who own their holiday homes.

many outdoor activities and games

Some of our parks are very lively and have ~~a great deal of entertainment~~ for children of all ages. On the other hand there are several parks that are peaceful and relaxing. Prospective buyers can stay one weekend in a caravan before deciding to buy. There is no charge for this, but anyone taking up this offer must prove a serious intent to purchase.

Refer to Resource Sheet and insert the paragraph on annual site fees here

We understand that purchasing a holiday caravan is a very large investment. However our finance packages can help to spread the cost over five years.

by having their finances in place

~~practical advice~~

We can offer you ~~useful help~~ about subletting your caravan. Subletting means you ⊘ can earn an extra income which can be used to offset your mortgage payments.

Contact Progress on 024 7647 0033 and arrange a visit to one of our parks. We have brochures for each park and we will be happy to send one to you.

Some of the running costs and

Print one copy displaying the track changes. Accept all changes and print a second copy which does not show the track changes.

RESOURCE SHEET

All holiday caravans are sold complete with furniture. Kitchens are equipped with fridges, freezers and cookers. Luxury caravans also have dishwashers and washing machines.

On new models, customers may choose from a selection of carpets and curtains.

Annual site fees vary according to which park you choose and the location of your caravan within the site. Other running costs include gas, electricity, water and general maintenance. Please refer to the brochures for the fees at each park.

EXERCISE WP 3.6

Recall the information sheet stored as TERMS and amend as shown ensuring that track changes are displayed. Display the whole document in 2 columns (newspaper style) each column 6.5 cm wide. Do not change font style or size and retain full justification.

TERMS AND CONDITIONS

designed to safeguard your personal details

SECURITY

As a customer using our online banking facilities, you are required to comply with certain security measures. Your security number must be kept safely and should never be divulged to another person. In telephone communications, our staff will never ask ~~you~~ for your security number.

If you receive a request for this information during a telephone call, terminate the call and ring our customer services on 0845 470033 *to report the incident.*

to our online service

Once you have logged on, you must not leave the terminal or allow another person to have access until you have logged off.

You must advise us immediately if you suspect that your account has been compromised in any way.

UNAUTHORISED TRANSACTIONS

fraudulent activities ✓

Any money taken from your account through ~~criminal methods~~ will be refunded in full *provided you have acted with reasonable care to ensure the safety of your security number and personal information.*

CHANGES AND LIABILITY

Refer to Resource Sheet and insert the paragraph on terms and conditions here

APPLICATIONS

We undertake to respond to any communication from you within 2 working days. You should telephone us if your request requires immediate action.

Any request for banking services should be directed to the relevant section on our website. This will ensure that you receive the correct information promptly.

decline any application that we think inappropriate

We reserve the right to ~~withdraw credit facilities if necessary.~~

You may be able to apply for credit facilities online.

Print one copy displaying the track changes. Accept all changes and print a second copy which does not show the track changes.

RESOURCE SHEET

Progress Internet Banking is a wholly owned subsidiary of Progress Banking plc. Its head office is situated at Progress House, Westwood Way, Coventry, CV4 8JQ. All transactions are authorised and regulated in compliance with standard banking criteria.

We reserve the right to alter our terms and conditions if necessary. Prior notification will be given 20 working days before any changes are made. We cannot be held liable for any loss caused by circumstances outside our control.

Online banking offers a flexible and convenient method for all your financial requirements.

TABLE

Layout

The table is designed to be displayed on a single sheet of A4 portrait paper. Use the tables function and work in *Print Layout View*.

Key each line horizontally, using the tab key or cursor to move between cells.

Ruling

The table should be ruled exactly as shown in the draft. If the gridlines are not showing, use **Format** ➤ **Borders and Shading** ➤ select **Gridlines**. You can call up the tables toolbar by using **View** ➤ **Toolbars** ➤ **Tables and Borders**. In some software versions gridlines can be switched on or off by selecting **Table** ➤ **Show/Hide gridlines**.

Headings

Follow capitalisation and layout exactly as given in the draft. Use **Table** ➤ **Merge Cells** to allow headings to cover more than one column.

Some headings will be vertical. To format these, key in the headings, select them and use **Format** ➤ **Text Direction** ➤ click the **Vertical** box under **Orientation**.

Align decimals

The decimal points in figures must be aligned. To set a decimal tab within the table, position your cursor in the place where you need the decimal tab, or select the whole column and click the tab selector on the far left of the top ruler line until ⊥ appears (indicates a decimal tab). Click on the ruler line at the point in the table where the decimal tab is required. Use the tab key to reach the decimal tab column and key in the figures, which should automatically align at the decimal point.

Incorporate information

You will be instructed to incorporate information from the Resource Sheet. Be careful to insert the necessary information only, keying in the details in the correct column order.

Sort columns

Highlight the sections of the table that need rearranging and use **Table** ➤ **Sort** ➤ **Ascending**. Make sure that all the corresponding details are also rearranged.

Modify layout

You are instructed to change the order of columns and sections. Use **Table** ➤ **Select Column** or **Select Row,** then use the cut and paste icons to insert the relevant text in its new position. Make sure you have left sufficient space in which to paste the selected text.

You will be instructed to modify the table by shading a section, removing lines or changing the style of lines. Use **Format** ➤ **Borders and Shading** ➤ select **Borders** or **Shading** as required. Print one copy of the table without these modifications and one showing the changes. Ensure that the text is legible when printed.

Proofread, checking that headings and columns are aligned consistently and that the correct details have been added.

EXERCISE WP 3.7

Key in the following table using Trebuchet Ms 10 font. Rule as shown. Refer to the Resource Sheet for completion of the table. Print one copy in portrait. Modify the table as instructed on the Resource Sheet. Print a second copy.

Modify layout so that HIGH OR LOW SEASON becomes the first column

PROGRESS HOLIDAY COTTAGES

COTTAGE DETAILS	TYPICAL COSTS		SLEEPS	HIGH OR LOW SEASON
	WEEKLY RENTAL £	ADDITIONAL CHARGES £		
Okehampton, Devon				
Forest Lodge has a sauna and spa bath. Barbecue available for hire.	1,250.00	10.00	10	High
Primrose Cottage is small but tastefully furnished. Accepts small dogs for daily charge.	500.00	3.50	4	High
Sunnyside Corner is delightful throughout the year. Horse riding charges are per person.	550.00	25.00	6	Low
Charmouth, Dorset				
Refer to Resource Sheet and incorporate the data for Charmouth, Dorset only to complete the table				
Charlestown, Cornwall				
The Sail Loft provides unusual accommodation. Owner has a dinghy for hire.	650.00	55.00	2	Low
Fisherman's Cottage next to the harbour. Daily fishing trips can be booked.	1,250.00	100.00	8	High

Sort WEEKLY RENTAL £ column into exact numerical order within each section starting with the highest. Ensure all corresponding details are also rearranged.

Modify layout so that Charlestown, Cornwall comes before Okehampton, Devon

RESOURCE SHEET

COTTAGE DETAILS	TYPICAL COSTS		SLEEPS	HIGH OR LOW SEASON
	WEEKLY RENTAL £	ADDITIONAL CHARGES £		
Charmouth, Dorset				
Sandy Villa sits on the beach. Diving equipment available.	1,000.00	40.00	10	Low
Rose Cottage is 2 miles from the village. Guided walks can be arranged.	1,500.00	20.00	8	High
Minehead, Somerset				
Moorland Rise is ideal for a relaxing break. Concessionary tickets to local attractions available.	500.00	7.50	Up to 6	Low
The Round House comprises very unusual accommodation. Windbreaks and other beach equipment for hire.	1,000.00	10.00	8-10	High
The Cedars, suitable for a family holiday. Totally safe for children. Cot available for hire for daily charge.	650.00	3.50	4	Low

TABLE MODIFICATION

Please add shading to the ADDITIONAL CHARGES £ column and change the outside border of the table to dashed line style as shown round this instruction. Print a second copy showing these modifications.

EXERCISE WP 3.8

> Key in the following table using Times New Roman font, point size 11. Rule as shown. Refer to the Resource Sheet for completion of the table. Print one copy in portrait. Modify the table as instructed on the Resource Sheet. Print a second copy.

> Modify the layout so that July to September section comes after April to June section.

BOOK PUBLICATIONS

The books that were published between January and September last year are listed below.

BOOK TITLE	DETAILS		TOTAL SOLD TO DATE	PRICE PER COPY £
	NAME OF AUTHOR	SECTION OR CATEGORY		
July to September				
My Life in Dorset	Andrew Hall	Biographical	114	13.29
The Pink Rose	Claire Patel	Romantic Fiction	967	8.50
Aliens from Distant Planets	Amanda Ling	Science Fiction	470	6.19
January to March				
Designs for Small Town Gardens	Jane Howe	Home and Garden	209	18.59
Paper Crafting for all Ages	Sally Wong	Arts and Crafts	107	7.89
Catering for Dinner Parties	Meena Ali	Food and Drink	308	15.99
April to June				
Refer to the Resource Sheet and incorporate the data for April to June only to complete the table.				

> Sort TOTAL SOLD TO DATE column into exact descending numerical order within each section. Ensure all corresponding details are also rearranged.

> Modify layout so that PRICE PER COPY £ becomes the first column

RESOURCE SHEET

BOOK TITLE	DETAILS		TOTAL SOLD TO DATE	PRICE PER COPY £
	NAME OF AUTHOR	SECTION OR CATEGORY		
April to June				
Creatures of the Deep Sea	Lee Jones	Natural History	217	17.19
Adventures in the Forest	Kevin Barnes	Children's Fiction	832	4.50
New Romantic Poems	Raj Bellman	Poetry and Drama	113	21.49
October to December				
French Phrase Book for Tourists	Simone Barr	Languages and Reference	367	9.99
Rules of International Hockey	Aiden Barker	Games and Sports	510	16.75
Laws Relating to Income Tax	Emily Morgan	Finance and Law	607	65.00

TABLE MODIFICATION

Please add shading to BOOK TITLE column and change all lines to dashed style as shown round this instruction. Print a second copy showing these modifications.

EXERCISE WP 3.9

Key in the following table using Century Gothic II font. Rule as shown. Refer to Resource Sheet for completion of the table. Print one copy in portrait. Modify the table as instructed on the Resource Sheet. Print a second copy.

Modify layout so that DESCRIPTION AND LOCATION OF PROPERTY becomes the first column

HOLIDAY AGENCY

Some owners pass on our commission charge to guests. Figures can be rounded up or down.

BROCHURE REFERENCE	NUMBER OF GUESTS	DESCRIPTION AND LOCATION OF PROPERTY	DETAILS OF CHARGES	
			WEEKLY RENTAL £	INCLUDING COMMISSION £
		Cumbria and Lancashire		
CLA	2	Annex with spacious accommodation near Clitheroe	415.00	480.41
CLEA	3	Elegant apartment with spectacular views near Penrith	780.00	902.95
CLTC	4	Traditional cottage near Ambleside with excellent amenities	595.00	688.78
		Refer to Resource Sheet and incorporate the data for Norfolk and Suffolk section only to complete the table		
		Devon and Somerset		
DCTV	5	Terraced Victorian house in Lanhydrock	685.00	792.97
DCTC	7	Thatched cottage on outskirts of Barnstaple	880.00	1018.71
DCLA	2	Luxury apartment in the Blackdown Hills	535.00	619.33

Sort WEEKLY RENTAL £ column into exact numerical order within each section starting with the lowest. Ensure all corresponding details are also rearranged.

Modify layout so that Devon and Somerset section comes before Cumbria and Lancashire section

25

RESOURCE SHEET

BROCHURE REFERENCE	NUMBER OF GUESTS	DESCRIPTION AND LOCATION OF PROPERTY	DETAILS OF CHARGES	
			WEEKLY RENTAL £	INCLUDING COMMISSION £
		Scotland		
SCB	5	Chalet bungalow near Strathdon	730.00	845.06
STSC	6	Terraced stone cottage by Loch Rannoch	675.00	781.40
SPA	4	Penthouse apartment near Aberdeen	960.00	1111.32
		Norfolk and Suffolk		
NSDH	8	Detached Elizabethan house in Wroxham with mooring	1225.00	1418.09
NSGFM	3	Ground floor maisonette near Thurgarton	425.00	491.99
NSBU	6	Beautifully presented bungalow in Blythburgh	865.00	1001.35

TABLE MODIFICATION

Please add shading to the DESCRIPTION AND LOCATION OF PROPERTY column and remove the NUMBER OF GUESTS column. Print a second copy showing these modifications.

BOOKLET/PROGRAMME/LEAFLET

Layout

This document is designed to be printed on two sides of A4 landscape paper, so that it can be folded to make a four-page booklet/leaflet.

To work in landscape use **File** ➤ **Page Setup** ➤ **Paper Size** ➤ choose **Landscape** and make sure you are in *Print Layout View*.

Follow instructions and complete the inside of the booklet/leaflet before starting a second page and keying in the front and back covers. Follow the order of the draft.

Formatting

You can use **File** ➤ **Page Setup** and on the Margins tab, in the Multiple pages section, select **2 pages per sheet** or **book fold** to create your booklet. Alternatively, you can use the columns facility; using **Format** ➤ **Columns** ➤ select **Two** ➤ make sure *Equal columns* is ticked. There is no need to number pages in this document. Note that some software may have different options. Consult the help pages of your software for information on how to do this.

Font

Details of the font style and size required for the main document are given to you. Make sure you change the recall text to match the font of your main document.

You will also be instructed to change the style or size of another section of text within this document.

Insert text

You are instructed to recall and copy part of a document to insert into this document. A simple way of doing this is to open the named file then select and copy the paragraphs required using the *Copy* icon. Close the stored file and return to your document, using the *Paste* icon to insert it into the correct position. Alter the style and size of font to match that of your main document.

Insert picture

You are required to choose a picture from three stored ones. Use the filename given to insert the correct picture in the position shown on the draft. To adjust the size, right click the picture and select **Format Picture** ➤ **Size** ➤ **Adjust height/width**.

Centre text

Use the *Centre* icon or **Ctrl + E** to centre the section of text over the typing line on the pages as indicated in the draft. Remember to return to left align at the end of that section.

Underline text

Use the *Underline* icon to underline the section of text indicated in the draft. Make sure that it does not extend to the spaces either side of the first and last word in the section.

Print

The best results are achieved by printing on both sides of one sheet of landscape paper, so that the text is the same way up on both sides and the document can be folded to make a four-page leaflet. However, you will not be penalised for printing out on two sides of A4 as long as as the orientation and position of pages are correct.

EXERCISE WP 3.10

Create this booklet using Comic Sans MS 11 font. This is the inside of the booklet. See overleaf for the outside.

Dogs are welcome free at many holiday properties, but it is generally best to check at the time of booking and if you have more than one dog you will need to obtain prior consent.

Where no charge is made for pets, any additional cleaning required will be the responsibility of the pet owner.

You are advised to bring your dog's own blanket or bed. In no circumstances should your pet be allowed on beds or furniture and never should your pet be left alone in the property. Please respect our clients' properties at all times.

Always ensure that your dog is not a nuisance to others. Do not let your pet wander away from your cottage to intimidate and annoy the residents of neighbouring properties.

Keep your dog under control and on a lead where requested.

If you follow these simple guidelines, you (and your dog) will be most welcome. Unfortunately it is the actions of the minority that create a problem for the rest.

Print this document on one or two sheets of plain A4 landscape. Ensure that the font style and size are consistent throughout except where indicated otherwise.

PET FRIENDLY COTTAGES

Copy the second paragraph of the document stored as DOGS and insert here

Insert the picture stored as CASSIE here. Adjust the size to 7 cm wide.

This is the front cover

Choose from one of our range of cottages or apartments situated close to great beaches, many of which are open all year round.

Give your dog a happy holiday too.

Centre this line

Check out our website for current details of holiday properties where dogs are welcome.

Emphasise this paragraph by changing the font style and size only

This is the back cover

EXERCISE WP 3.11

Create this booklet using Trebuchet MS font, point size 14. This is the inside of the booklet. See overleaf for the outside.

Copy the third paragraph of the document stored as HALLS and insert here

The college has won many awards for its innovative teaching methods. The majority of students who obtain professional qualifications start their careers with good jobs and earn high salaries.

We have some modern facilities and offer students all the advice and support needed in order to help them pass their final examinations.

The bookshop on campus stocks the books and stationery appropriate for all of the courses held at The Green Campus. At times there are second-hand copies of most course books available for purchase. These are being sold by past students and the price of these varies according to the age and condition of the book.

Careers guidance officers are happy to give impartial and confidential advice to students on job hunting and interview techniques.

Some students may be able to get financial assistance with course materials and travelling costs. For details please contact George Ahmed in the college finance department.

Print this document on one or two sheets of plain A4 paper landscape. Ensure that the font style and size are consistent throughout except where indicated otherwise

this is the front cover

PROGRESS TECHNICAL COLLEGE

The Green Campus
Hazelmere Road
BASINGSTOKE
Hampshire
RG21 4AA

Telephone 01256 814973

Below is a list of courses
available at this campus.

Art and design
Construction and engineering
Travel and tourism
Business and management

*Change font style and size
for this section only*

this is the back cover

PROGRESS EDUCATION

Insert the picture stored
as COLLEGE here. Adjust
the size to 6.5cm high

See below for a list of
the other colleges
administered by Progress.

Sutton Coldfield
Milton Keynes
Great Yarmouth
Newton Abbot
Wootton Bassett
Saffron Walden

Centre this section

EXERCISE WP 3.12

Create this leaflet using Arial 14 font. This is the inside of the leaflet. See overleaf for the outside.

Day 1

Our tour guide will meet you on arrival. There may be a short delay whilst he locates all the members of the party who will be travelling in various parts of the train.

Copy the first and second paragraphs of the document stored as JOURNEY and insert here

Day 2

Following a delicious Continental breakfast, you will be taken by coach on a sightseeing tour visiting almost all the famous landmarks.

Day 3

This is a more leisurely day. You may decide to visit a museum or art gallery or take a relaxing boat trip along the River Seine.

In the evening, you have the opportunity to see Paris by night with its glorious illuminations.

Day 4

There will be time in the morning to shop for mementos or you may decide to walk in the nearby park.

The coach will deliver you to the station in time for your departure.

Print this document on one or two sheets of plain A4 landscape. Ensure that the font style and size are consistent throughout except where indicated otherwise.

INFORMATION FOR PARIS

This leaflet provides details of your itinerary.

Insert the picture stored as TOWER here. Adjust the size to 8 cm high.

Tour Operator: Progress Continental Travel
Accommodation: Hotel Soleil
Tour Guide: Percy Grigson

Centre these lines

This is the front cover

The most convenient way to explore Paris and the surrounding area is by the metro system. Our guide will give you a comprehensive map with information on the nearest station to your hotel.

You can make a considerable saving by buying a book of 10 tickets.

Emphasise this sentence by changing the font style and size only

Remember to bring comfortable footwear with you.

This is the back cover

AUDIO-TRANSCRIPTION LEVEL 3 PRACTICE EXERCISES

WITH DETAILED NOTES ON HOW TO WORK THE FOLLOWING DOCUMENTS:

- Letter
- Minutes
- Advertisement
- Itinerary
- Report
- Article

LETTER

Layout and style

For a reminder of layout and style refer to the Text Production notes on business letters (page 48). Unless stated otherwise, the same rules apply to Audio-Transcription.

Candidate Information Sheet

The Candidate Information Sheet contains references, names, addresses and proper nouns. This is to help you with the spelling of such words.

Reference

You will be given an *Our ref* and may also be given a *Your ref*. Key in the references exactly as shown on the reference sheet with regard to spacing, punctuation and capitalisation. Do not add your initials to a reference, as this will incur a penalty.

Date

You must date this document with the date on which you work it. See the detailed notes under Text Production (page 49).

Correction to text

Listen for the word correction and key the substituted word.

Special mark

You will be instructed to insert a special mark in closed capitals.

Heading

Follow capitalisation and underlining as dictated.

Punctuation

Most essential punctuation is dictated, except for the end of a paragraph when the word *paragraph* will indicate a final full stop followed by a clear linespace.

You may need to insert an apostrophe in the text to make it grammatically correct. This will not be dictated.

Enclosure

You will need to indicate the enclosure(s) mentioned in the body of the letter. At this level you must show whether there are single or multiple enclosures.

Copies and routing

You will be instructed to print two extra copies of this document and indicate the routing. Follow the instructions given in the Text Production business letter notes (page 50).

You may print extra copies and make routing ticks in ink outside the exam time allocation, but you may not key in the copy details at that stage.

Accessing audio exercises material

Candidate Information Sheets

Candidate Information Sheets follow for exercises:

- AT 3.1
- AT 3.2
- AT 3.3

Templates

The letter template is available on the Hodder Plus website at **www. hodderplus.co.uk/ocrtextprocessing**. The same template can be used for all exercises.

Dictated documents

The dictation for the above exercises is available on the Hodder Plus website.

EXERCISE AT 3.1

CANDIDATE INFORMATION SHEET

Included in dictation:

Paul Jennings
European
European Union
Switzerland
Mandeep Bhalay
Card Issue Office
Brenda Coles

References:

MB/RF

Address:

18 Randall Avenue
MIDDLESBROUGH
TS2 4EJ

NB: **All other instructions (eg courtesy titles, special mark, extra copies, headings etc) will be given in the dictation.**

EXERCISE AT 3.2

CANDIDATE INFORMATION SHEET

Included in dictation:

Benedict Humphries
Giles Gillespie
Customer Account Team
Rupinder Gupta

Address:

9 Apple Grove
UPWEY
Dorset
DT3 4AG

Reference(s):

GG/BC

NB: All other instructions (eg courtesy titles, headings, etc) will be given in the dictation.

EXERCISE AT 3.3

CANDIDATE INFORMATION SHEET

Included in dictation:

Edward Greatorex
Ann Foster
Listed Buildings Officer
David Palmer

Reference:

AF/LA

Address:

34 Trent Gardens
LEAMINGTON SPA
CV31 8HQ

NB: All other instructions (og courtesy titles, special mark, extra copies, headings etc) will be given in the dictation.

MINUTES/ADVERTISEMENT/ITINERARY

None of these documents should be dated. Key in the text, carrying out the one-word correction as dictated.

Punctuation

Most essential punctuation is dictated, except for the end of a paragraph when the word *paragraph* will indicate a final full stop followed by a clear linespace.

You may need to insert an apostrophe in the text to make it grammatically correct. This will not be dictated.

Headings

Follow the style dictated for headings and subheadings throughout the document.

Emphasis

You will be instructed to emphasise a heading, paragraph or sentence. You may embolden, capitalise, underline, alter font style/size, centre or inset. Remember to take the emphasis instruction off at the end of the portion of text.

Centre

You will be instructed to centre an item of text. To do so, highlight it and use the *Centre* icon. Remember to return to left align for the rest of the document.

Vertical space

You are required to leave a vertical space of a specified measurement within the text. A simple way to do this is to make sure you are in *Print Layout View*, then use *Enter* to create sufficient hard returns to leave the clear linespaces needed. Check the measurement against the ruler line at the far left of your screen.

The measurement is taken from the bottom of the last line of text before the space to the top of the first line of text after the space.

Accessing audio exercises material

Candidate Information Sheets

Candidate Information Sheets follow for exercises:

AT 3.4
AT 3.5
AT 3.6
AT 3.7
AT 3.8
AT 3.9

AT 3.10
AT 3.11
AT 3.12

Dictated documents

The dictation for the above exercises is available on the Hodder Plus website at
www.hodderplus.co.uk/ocrtextprocessing.

EXERCISE AT 3.4

CANDIDATE INFORMATION SHEET

Included in dictation:

Hillside Housing Association
Somerfield
Treasurer
Chairman
Edinburgh

References:

Address:

NB: All other instructions (eg courtesy titles, special mark, extra copies, headings etc) will be given in the dictation.

EXERCISE AT 3.5

CANDIDATE INFORMATION SHEET

Included in dictation:

Frobisher Windows Ltd
Westcott House
Wessex Bank
Hoggs Bank
Blaise Kingsley
Indemnity Insurance Company Ltd

Address:

Reference(s):

NB: All other instructions (eg courtesy titles, headings, etc) will be given in the dictation.

EXERCISE AT 3.6

CANDIDATE INFORMATION SHEET

Included in dictation:

Shardwell County Offices
Ann Foster
Imran Hussain
Paula Henriques
Julie Wood

Reference:

Address:

NB: All other instructions (eg courtesy titles, special mark, extra copies, headings etc) will be given in the dictation.

EXERCISE AT 3.7

CANDIDATE INFORMATION SHEET

Included in dictation:

Mariella Lynch
m.lynch@progress.ac.uk

References:

Address:

NB: All other instructions (eg courtesy titles, special mark, extra copies, headings etc) will be given in the dictation.

EXERCISE AT 3.8

CANDIDATE INFORMATION SHEET

Included in dictation:

United Kingdom
CV

Address:

Reference(s):

NB: All other instructions (eg courtesy titles, headings, etc) will be given in the dictation.

EXERCISE AT 3.9

CANDIDATE INFORMATION SHEET

Included in dictation:

Stephanie Morrow
Human Resources

Reference:

Address:

NB: All other instructions (og courtesy titles, special mark, extra copies, headings etc) will be given in the dictation.

EXERCISE AT 3.10

CANDIDATE INFORMATION SHEET

DOCUMENT 2

Included in dictation:

Ireland
Stansted
Sarah O'Donnell
Dublin
Sales Manager

References:

Address:

NB: **All other instructions (eg courtesy titles, special mark, extra copies, headings etc) will be given in the dictation.**

EXERCISE AT 3.11

CANDIDATE INFORMATION SHEET

Included in dictation:

Court Hotel
Weymouth

Address:

Reference(s):

NB: All other instructions (eg courtesy titles, headings, etc) will be given in the dictation.

EXERCISE AT 3.12

CANDIDATE INFORMATION SHEET

Included in dictation:

East Midlands Airport
Charles De Gaulle Airport
Paris
United Kingdom

Reference:

Address:

NB: All other instructions (eg courtesy titles, special mark, extra copies, headings etc) will be given in the dictation.

REPORT/ARTICLE

Key in the text, carrying out the one-word corrections as dictated. You should not date this document.

Headings

Follow capitalisation for the main heading and text in the body of the letter as dictated. You may display the subheadings and table column headings in a style of your choice.

Page numbering

Continuation pages should be numbered in this multi-page document.

Numbered paragraphs

A list of items will be dictated. You can key the numbers as you go, using the tab key to align the following text, or you can key in the list, highlight it and use **Format** ➤ **Bullets and Numbering** ➤ select **Numbered**. This will insert numbers and align the text automatically.

Linespacing

There will be an instruction to alter linespacing for several paragraphs of text. Make sure that the spacing between paragraphs is consistent. Do not forget to change back to the original linespacing at the end of that section.

Distraction element

In the Audio-Transcription exam, an item of extra information is given to you. It is to be included in this document and the dictation will tell you where to insert it. For the practice exercises you will find the relevant information on the accompanying separate sheet.

Table

This document will include a table. Column widths are dictated for candidates keying the table using the tab key. The following hints apply to those using the tables function.

- Working in *Print Layout View*, key each line horizontally – using the tab key or cursors to move between cells.
- Column widths can be altered to your requirements by dragging the column borders with the mouse.
- Extra linespaces can be inserted by pressing Enter from within the cell.
- Gridlines may be used in the table, but a clear linespace should be left below the column headings. To stop the gridlines from printing use **Format** ➤ **Borders and Shading** ➤ **Borders** select **None**. Do not leave empty cells.

- To set a decimal tab, position your cursor in the place where you need the decimal tab, or select the whole column and click the tab selector on the far left of the top ruler line until ⊥ appears (shows decimal tab). Click the ruler line at the point in the table where the decimal tab is required. Use the tab key to reach the decimal tab column and key in the figures, which should automatically align at the decimal point.

Accessing audio exercises material

Candidate Information Sheets

Candidate Information Sheets follow for exercises:

- AT 3.13
- AT 3.14
- AT 3.15

Dictated documents

The dictation for the above exercises is available on the Hodder Plus website at **www.hodderplus.co.uk/ocrtextprocessing**.

EXERCISE AT 3.13

CANDIDATE INFORMATION SHEET

DOCUMENT 3

Included in dictation:

Retail Price Index

References:

Address:

NB: All other instructions (eg courtesy titles, special mark, extra copies, headings etc) will be given in the dictation.

INSTRUCTIONS TO INVIGILATOR:

About 15-30 minutes after the start of the examination, announce that for

Document 3:

flexible working has now been extended to apply to all employees who have

responsibility for a child under the age of seventeen

EXERCISE AT 3.14

CANDIDATE INFORMATION SHEET

Included in dictation:

Address:

Reference(s):

NB: All other instructions (eg courtesy titles, headings, etc) will be given in the dictation.

INSTRUCTIONS FOR INVIGILATOR

About 15 – 30 minutes after the start of the examination, announce that for Document 3

business contacts are a good sign of how the company is viewed.

EXERCISE AT 3.15

CANDIDATE INFORMATION SHEET

Included in dictation:

Ashman Brothers
Gibson and Green
Stronghill Ltd
Cross Company Limited
Garcia Brothers
Lock plc

Reference:

Address:

NB: All other Instructions (eg courtesy titles, special mark, extra copies, headings
       etc) will be given in the dictation.

INSTRUCTIONS FOR INVIGILATOR

About 15-30 minutes after the start of the examination, announce that for Document 3

a close check is kept on customers who have failed to settle their account within the

sixty day period allowed.

EXAM WORK

4

This section provides hints for exam work, together with three new practice exams for each unit, similar to the OCR standard. The hints and complete exams for each different unit are grouped together.

Hints pages

Hints pages precede each set of exams. They remind you of the skills you will have acquired in the practice exercises and of the methods you can use to complete each exam successfully. Take the time to read the hints relating to each unit before attempting the exam in that subject. You can refer to the hints as you work through each practice exam. *Of course, you may not refer to the notes or hints in this book at the time of sitting the real exams.*

Practice exams

There are three new complete practice exams for each unit. Recall text for these exams is available on the Hodder Plus website (see below). Once you have finished a complete exam, proofread it and correct any errors. Make sure you have saved the final version of each document, using the filenames indicated, and print copies. Find the correct worked example of the exam in the 'Worked Examples' section on the Hodder Plus website and proofread your copy against this. If you are a member of a group, you may find it helpful to proofread each other's work, or your tutor may wish to take in your work for marking.

Recall text from the Hodder Plus website

You will need to access files on the Hodder Plus website at **www.hodderplus.co.uk/ocrtextprocessing** in order to carry out the following:

- open and use letterhead and fax templates
- recall text and amend as instructed
- access worked examples for all exams.

The templates that you will need to recall are saved under the following filenames:

> LETTERHEAD
> FAX

The text that you will need to recall for Word Processing is saved under the filenames given to you in each document in the practice exercises and exams.

Audio-Transcription

The Candidate Information Sheets (containing proper nouns) and Instruction to Invigilator Sheets (with information for document 3) are provided in this section. Dictated material is saved under filenames given to each exercise and accessed from the Hodder Plus website at **www.hodderplus.co.uk/ ocrtextprocessing**.

TEXT PRODUCTION LEVEL 3 PRACTICE EXAMS

WITH HINTS SHEETS COVERING

- Skills Checklist
- General Hints
- Hints for Each Document

HINTS FOR EXAM WORK: OCR TEXT PRODUCTION LEVEL 3

Checklist of skills

You need to be able to carry out the following before you attempt the practice exams:

- recall and use a letterhead and fax
- lay out a letter and insert a special mark
- alter linespacing
- inset text from left margin
- emphasise, centre and underline text and headings
- insert and delete text
- create new paragraphs, insert and close up spaces
- interpret and carry out amendment and correction signs
- expand abbreviations from OCR list
- spell words from OCR list of business vocabulary
- identify and correct typographical and grammatical errors
- identify and correct punctuation errors
- select and incorporate information from a Resource Sheet
- present information in tables format
- indicate single and multiple enclosure(s)
- add automatic page numbering
- insert footnotes

- rearrange numbered items
- number continuation sheets.

General

- Start a **New** file for each document.
- You may use either the **Header** or **Footer** facility to record your name, centre number and document number on each printout.
- Recall a letterhead or fax template then use **Save As** to give it a filename. The templates are available on the Hodder Plus website at **www.hodderplus.co.uk/ocrtextprocessing**.
- Thereafter click on the **Save** screen icon frequently as you work.
- As a general rule for these exam units, carry out editing instructions as you key in, apart from linespacing and vertical spacing instructions, which can be left to the end.
- As you complete each instruction, tick it off on the question paper. This makes it easier to keep track, particularly when working on a multi-paged document. However, it may not be appropriate to mark the textbook unless it is your own property.
- As you key in an email or internet address, your computer changes the text colour to blue and underscores it. It can be left like this.
- You may print as often as you wish, both during and immediately after the exam time allocation. However, remember that the process is time-consuming, particularly when many candidates are involved, so you should proofread carefully from the screen prior to printing.
- Proofread a second time from the hard copy.
- **Ensure you have SAVED your final edited version of each document before you log off at the end of the session.**

Document 1: letter

- This document must be printed on the OCR letterhead template.
- It must be dated with the date you are doing the practice exam.
- Key in references exactly as shown. Do not add your own initials.
- Key the special mark immediately before the name and address.
- Remember to include the subject heading after the salutation.
- Key in text, making amendments according to the draft.
- Follow draft for capitalisation.
- Spelling and typographical errors should be identified and corrected by you. They are not circled at this level.
- Punctuation and grammatical errors should be identified and corrected by you. They are not circled at this level.

- Abbreviations, which are not circled, should be identified by you and expanded. Abbreviations that do not appear on the list given in the assessment criteria section, such as Ltd, plc, NB, etc should not be expanded.
- Use a calendar or diary to check the date for the postdating item. Only the day and month are essential. It is not necessary to include the year.
- When incorporating information from the Resource Sheet, make sure you have included all the required words.
- Do not number single-page documents, but continuation sheets must be numbered. Use **Insert → Page Numbers** to customise your numbering.
- Remember to show whether any enclosure is single or multiple.
- Proofread carefully and use the **Spellcheck**, and check that you have not omitted or misplaced text.

Document 2: fax/minutes/terms of reference/contract

- You must use the fax template provided and insert the details alongside the appropriate headings. The minutes, terms of reference and contract do not have template headings and should be keyed on plain A4 paper.
- Key in text, making amendments according to the draft. Linespacing alterations may be left to the end.
- You must insert the date on which you are doing the practice exam on the fax.
- Follow draft for capitalisation.
- Spelling and apostrophe errors should be identified and corrected by you. They are not circled at this level.
- Abbreviations, which are not circled, should be identified by you and expanded. Abbreviations that do not appear on the list given in the assessment criteria section, such as Ltd, plc, NB, etc should not be expanded.
- When incorporating information from the Resource Sheet, make sure you have included all the required words.
- Remember to rearrange the three items in the numbered list. It is simple to key them in the correct order as you go.
- When keying the table, remember to leave a clear linespace between headings and the first row of text. Ruling should not be shown in the printout.
- You may be required to indicate an attachment to any of these documents.
- Proofread carefully and use the **Spellcheck**, and check that you have not omitted or misplaced text.

Document 3: report/article

- Key in text, making amendments according to the draft. Linespacing alterations may be left to the end.
- Follow draft for capitalisation.

- Spelling and typographical errors should be identified and corrected by you. They are not circled at this level.
- Punctuation and apostrophe errors should be identified and corrected by you. They are not circled at this level.
- Abbreviations, which are not circled, should be identified by you and expanded. Abbreviations that do not appear on the list given in the assessment criteria section, such as Ltd, plc, NB, etc should not be expanded.
- When transposing items vertically, be careful to switch the position of the circled words only, eg if only the paragraph headings are circled, the headings should be switched, but the paragraphs left in their original order. Be especially careful not to omit any intervening text.
- When insetting text you must do so using the exact measurement given. Highlight the section, then use **Format** → **Paragraph** → **Indents and Spacing** → select **Indentation Left** → key in the correct measurement.
- Single-page documents should not be numbered, but continuation sheets must be numbered. **Insert** → **Page Numbers** will allow you to customise your numbering.
- To insert a footnote use **Insert** → **Footnote and Endnote** → select **Footnote** and **Autonumber** → **OK**. The footnote must appear on the same page as the original indication in the text. Use the help factility of your package if your software version differs from this.
- When incorporating information from the Resource Sheet, make sure you have included all the required words.
- Proofread carefully and use the **Spellcheck**, and check that you have not omitted or misplaced text.

EXAM TP 3.A1

Letter to Mrs E Collins 27 Elm Sq PEWSEY Wiltshire SN9 3FH Our ref AJ/LN Please use the heading OFFICE MANAGER

Your ref EP/43

Mark this URGENT

Dear Mrs Collins

Thank you for attending ~~these premises~~ this office last Tuesday for ✓ an interview for the position of office manager. I was very impressed with your experiense and I would like to offer you this position. // I explained to you that our last office manager had to retire suddenly due to ill health. Therefore I need you to start work asap. I understand that your current position is a temperary one and that your contract is due to finish next week. i would like your employment with us to commence on Monday (give date for first Monday of next month)

I enclose two copies of your employment contract and your job description. Each document requires your sig and you should return one copy of each to me. The second copy is for your record's. I am also enclosing a brochure called (please insert name of brochure here) and this will give you additional info about the business.

When you have worked for us for six month you will be able to join our pension scheme. My sec will provide you with a complete list of benefits. The reason that we provide extra benefits are to help all of our employees.

I hope that the terms of this offer is acceptable to you.

Yours sncly , our branch office and products

Anthea Jones
Personnel Manager

EXAM TP 3.A2

PROGRESS GROUP

(PROVISIONS AND LIMITATIONS)
(TRAINING CONTRACT)

The terms ~~and conditions~~ of the contract are given in this doc. The trainee shall agree to:

1	attend classes punctually
4 ~~2~~	follow all instructions carefully
2 ~~3~~	tel if unable to attend classes
3 ~~4~~	submit assignments on time
5	carry out routine office tasks as necy
6	dress appropriately for a bussiness environment

(Emphasise this sentence only)

Trainees will be personally responsable for all equipment issued to them.

                          for training fees
The repayment schedule / is set out below.

PAYMENT	MONTH	AMOUNT PAYABLE
1	March	no more than five per cent of pay
2	June	ten per cent of pay
3	Sept	half the outstanding sum
4	December	all remaining fees

The trainee shall undertake to work for Progress for a minimum of one yr after completing the course.

(If the trainee leaves before this time all outstanding fees become payable _immediately_.

✓ ~~Trainees~~
~~Employees~~ are guaranteed (at the end of the course) a job with Progress. Details of employment opportunities can be found in the booklet called C_____ Prospects.

Successful course completion is assessed by monthly tests. The pass mark for tests and examination's is set at eighty per cent.

(an examination at the end of the course and by)

EXAM TP 3.A3

(double linespacing except where indicated)

PROGRESS GROUP HOTELS ◄——— (Centre this heading)

REFURBISHED CONFERENCE CENTRE

We are ~~happy that our new centre is ready to be opened~~. pleased to announce the opening of a new conference centre During the past six months we have been unable to accomodate clients who have asked to use this centre because of the extensive refurbishments which were taking place. We will be open at the beginning of next month and we are offering past clients a discount of twenty per cent on their first booking in the new centre. Terms and conditions will apply to the discount. For further info please tel the Progress Group on 024 7647 0033 and we will send you a brochure. Alternatively you can visit our web site where you will be able to view photographs and floor plans* of both the conference rooms in the new centre.

The hotel is located on the outskirt6s of Chippenham which is a busy market town and has good shopping facilities. The hotel is easily accessible by train, bus and road. It is a short taxi ride from the main railway station and just a few miles from the motor way junction. Additionally, we have a large car park with sufficient space for up to two hundred cars.

CATERING FACILITIES

(as frequently as required throughout the day)

We can provide food and drink for a wide range of tastes and budgets. Delegates are able to sit together ~~in the conference centre restaurant~~ and do not have to dine with other hotel guests in the main restaurant. The catering dept can provide clients with ——— ——— for breakfast, lunch and dinner. A selection of teas, coffees, biscuits and cakes can be provided.

* showing theatre and classroom layouts

BEDROOMS

(these paragraphs only in single line spacing)

All our luxury bedrooms have private bathrooms which are fitted with seperate shower cubicles and spa baths. <u>Writing desks and internet access are standard features</u> in all bedrooms. [We have a few luxury suites which are situated on the top floor of the hotel and the views from all the suites are stunning.

On the ____ side of the hotel the views are over open countryside and woodland, and on the north side there are views across the town to the river Avon. There are a few suites with views over our beautiful gardens.

MEETING ROOM ONE

OUr first meeting room has seating for up two hundred people when the room is set out in a theatre style. There is also a ~~large lecture~~ table on a raised platform with seating for several speakers.

When the room is set out as a clasroom with delegates sitting at tables the capacity will be reduced.

MEETING ROOM TWO

is ideal for smaller groups
This ~~room is suitable for smaller meetings with fewer speakers and delegates~~.
There is no platform so the speakers and delegates can be placed in any locatoin.

EQUIPMENT

Inset this paragraph 50mm from left margin

Whatever you plan to do in the conferences we can provide the equipment you need. We have a good range of both audio and visual equipment. Should you require additional items we can obtian almost any item for you. Our standard equipment** can be setup in either of the two meeting rooms.

RECEPTION

We can provide a receptionist to greet people on their arrrival and to distribute badges for an extra charge.

We are very happy to provide name badges for everyone who is attending. Clients may choose the style and colour of badge from our brochure. all we require is a complete list of attendees a minimum of three day's before the conference date.

The new centre has its own reception room and this is a large rooom with comfortable chairs and tables where people can meet and talk. Clients can use the reception to put up exhibits in some of the free space

BOOKINGS

Julie Dunne, who is the manager, will be pleased to discuss yr needs. She has a great deal of experience running conference centres, hotels and offices and can offer advice to clients. Julie will do all she can to ensure that the conference is a huge success.

** complete list in our brochure

Document 1

Letter

The company brochure which is called Progress International Business Group gives details about the business, its products and services.

Document 2

Contract

Employment opportunities with this company are described in detail in the booklet entitled Career Prospects.

Document 3

Article

Views over open countryside and woodland can be seen from the south side of the hotel.

Views across the town to the river Avon can be seen from the north side of the hotel.

Simple or gourmet menus can be provided for breakfast, lunch and dinner.

Standard features in all bedrooms are writing desks and internet access.

EXAM TP 3.B1

Letter to Mr T R Hopkirk 60 Gloucester Ave HAUGHLEY Suffolk IP14 8JV Our ref AM/pcc Please use the heading MANAGING YOUR SHARES

Your ref 44931

Mark this CONFIDENTIAL

Dear Mr Hopkirk

In our letter last month, we informed you of a new service that we would be introducing to our shareholders. The aims of this service is to give you further info about your shares and also about the ways in which we can help you to manage your ~~investment money~~.

At the top of the attached form we give you an approx guide as to what your shares are now worth. the market fluctuates daily, so As you will apreciate, it is poss that the value of your shares are less than you paid for them. You have the opp to sell some, or all of your holding. If you would like to do this, please complete the attachment. Should you wish to donate (please insert what you are donating and to whom here), please tick the appropriate box. Alternatively, you may decide to buy some additional shares, in which case please fill in the relevant section of the attachment and return it with your cheque by Friday (give date for last Friday of next month). There is an administrative fee for this.

Finally, if none of these option's appeals to you, there are no need to take any action The service will remain available to you should you change your mind in the future.

Please contact us if you have any queries.

Yours sncly

Andrew Manthorpe
Finnance Manager

EXAM TP 3.B2

> 1 page fax from John Harrold to Melanie Catchpole
> at Busproms plc, ref JH/25cel, fax number 01222 417254

Our company was established 25 years ago and is planning
to celebrate its anniversary with a champagne reception.
The Board of Director's would like to give promotional gifts
at this event.   *to all its valued customers*

emphasise this line →

We have selected the following misc items from your cat:

Item	Description	Quantity	Page
Foldable desk clock	With calendar and alarm	250	41
Eco friendly ball pen	biodegradable	1000	29
LED key ring light	extra bright bulb	1000	65
Executive wine stopper	brushed silver finish	100	132

Further info on the points listed below would be ~~helpful~~ useful: ✓

1   product cost
2   VAT
3   maximum print area
5 ~~4~~   artwork ~~cost origination~~
6 ~~5~~   carriage cost
4 ~~6~~   c_____ logo
7   approx timescale for delivery

The intention of our celebration is, of course, to project a
favourable image *to our customers* ~~of our company~~. With your
long experience in marketing, we should appreciate your
guidance in this matter.

I should like to arrange a mtg with you to discuss the above
and, if possible, to see some samples *of the above items* ~~before~~ placing an order.

> Please let me know if you are available sometime next week.

EXAM TP 3.B3

Double linespacing except where indicated

PROGRESS BANKING GROUP ← centre this heading

Progress Banking Group was set up over 20 years ago. We provide a wide range of banking services to individuals, businesses and charitable orgs. We offer an ethical approach to banking. Therefore, we will only lend money to companies and charities that aim to benefit society and the environment. We have many thousands of shareholders and offices throughout Europe and clients worldwide.

In the current climate we believe that it is more important than ever to express our concern over issues such as global warming and other social and enviromental problems. Recently, over _____ customers filled in a questionnaire and, interestingly, their views refflected these same concerns. Afterall it is our customers money that we invest, so they should have a say in where it ends up!

Inset these paragraphs 30 mm from the left margin

Progress Bank helps to fund charitable projects, not only here. In the United ＊, but also overseas
Kingdom one of its projects has helped to porvide housing for homeless families and children. Another scheme has enabled children of school age and parents to acess an educational website free of charge. ＊

Overseas projects include supplying basic financial help to poor people and lending money to buy land. Families can then set up their own small businesses by growing fruit and vegetables. Alternatively, they could buy a goat or chickens. Eventually, in this way, some of the loan can be repaid. This gives people a feeling of independence and can often change their lives.

＊ linked to the National Curriculum

Investment Banking

This section only in single linespacing

Our bank provides a full range of services to businesses and charities as long as
they value society and the plannet. We provide current and deposit accounts as well
as loans. Our expeirenced and dedicated team will work with companies to provide
corporate banking. Our on line banking will also allow customers the flexib8ility to
manage their money at any time of the day or night.

We also have overdraft
facilities.

Personal Banking

For those people who wish to feel that their money is making a real change to
lives, we will link you to like-minded companies. At the same time your money will
be earning interest. We have a full range of personal savings accounts. Whether
you have a lump sum to invest or whether you wish to save a small amuont each
month, we have the right savings account for you.

Business and Charity Banking

There is a zealous investment dept that has worked
with a number of leading ethical businesses. As climate
change is an important issue for us, we advise firms
on financing renewable energy schemes.

Terms and Conditions

Progress Banking Group is a member of ⸺ ⸺ ⸺.
This sets the standards of good banking practice in this
country. Our ethical policy ensures that we handle all
~~We therefore offer a very high standard of~~
complaints in a fair and non-biased way.
~~service to all our customers~~

The following summary of our terms and conditions applies to all business, charity
and personal bank accounts. To open an account with us you must provide proof of

identity ** of those managing the account   We will also need to know the nature of the business. This is a legal requirement and will protect you as well as our banking group. ONce the account is opened, you may pay money in by bank giro credit or by post with a paying-in slip. Your money will then start increasing. You may withdraw by standing order , direct debit or by cheque. There is a free cheque allowance for all charity accounts.

~~A fee is charged for stopping cheques~~ Any alterations to your account details must be sent to our head office in writing with the approved sigs, in accordance with your mandate. If you wish to have overdraft facilities, please contact us.

For those with an internet account security may be a worry, ~~Precautions should be taken if you are opening an online account~~ in which case we will give you some simple guidlines.

For further information on any of the above services, please ~~visit our website or~~ tel us.

** a passport or driving licence is acceptable

RESOURCE SHEET

DOCUMENT 1

Letter

Our new service to shareholders gives them the choice of buying some more shares, or selling their existing shares. In this case, shareholders may choose to donate the proceeds to charity if they so wish.

DOCUMENT 2

Fax

The company is celebrating 25 years since it was set up and would like clarification on a number of points about the promotional gifts it plans to give to its customers at the champagne reception. One of the queries is whether its corporate logo can be printed on the chosen gift. A meeting is to be arranged to discuss this and a number of other issues.

DOCUMENT 3

Article

Progress Banking Group offers an ethical approach to banking. Over 100,000 customers completed a questionnaire and their views also showed concerns over global warming and other environmental problems.

Progress Banking Group subscribes to The Banking Code which sets the standards of good banking practice in this country.

EXAM TP 3.C1

Letter to Mr and Mrs J Clowes   46 Madison Ave
WHITEFIELD   Greater Manchester   M46 7YX
Our ref TR/219   Please use the heading YOUR PROPERTY

Your ref   CL32

Mark this URGENT

Dear Mr and Mrs Clowes

It was good to meet you yesterday and to have an opp to inspect your property with a view to adding it to our rental portfolio. [Your house is located in a part of Greater Manchester which are very popular with commuters. The off-road parking and proximity to good schools and transport links makes it a very good option for families. With its two reception rooms and four bedrooms, I would suggest that a rental of give details here could be acheeved.

At our meeting you mentioned that you will be moving to Scotland for a two-year work contract. As your new job will start on Monday give date for first Monday of next month), we must move quickly if we are to get tenant's in place by that date

✓ You could rent your property for the ~~whole period~~ entire time or you might choose to start with a twelve-month tenancy agreement. Please let me know which option you prefer.

For your information, our letting fee are ▼ £150 per month. We will advetise your property, find suitable tenants, undertake the new financial checks and collect the rent each month.

Please tel on the above number to confirm that you wish to proceed. I look forward to hearing from you.

Yrs sncly

10% of the rental or

Tanya Robinson
Lettings Manager

EXAM TP 3.C2

(Please emphasise this sentence)

MINUTES OF MEETING

→ A short meeting of the Lettings Team was held in the Conf Room.

ATTENDANCE   Tanya Robinson   Manager
         (Rupert Wilson)   Senior Lettings Executive
         (Hansa Divani)   Lettings Executive
         Sam Westcote   Administrative Assistant

(at 1030 on Friday 3 May)

APOLOGIES FOR ABSENCE

(✓) Apologies were recieved from Manuel Rojas who was on ~~Paternity~~ ~~Annual~~ leave ~~for two weeks.~~

MINUTES OF LAST MEETING   by all present

The minutes of the previous meeting were accepted/and signed by Tanya.

RECENT TRENDS

Hansa reported that there had been an upturn in the number of requests for residential lettings over the past month. She attributed this to an improvement in the emp situation.

Rupert added that his figures reflected the same increase.

TRAINEE

Tanya confirmed that Jo H___ would be joining the Dept (on a temp six-month contract) as a trainee). She would start as soon as poss. Her role would be to

1   shadow Hansa and Rupert on visits to properties
3,2   prepare draft tenancy agreements
4,3   assist Sam with administrative tasks
2,4   maintain the cleint database

Jos' contract would be extended if the trial period proved to be a success.

DATE OF NEXT MEETING

The next meeting would be held at 1100 on Friday 21 June.

EXAM TP 3.C3

Double linespacing except where indicated

PROGRESS PROPERTIES

THE LETTING GAME

Centre these headings

In times when a downturn in the economy means that fewer people are prepared to move house, one alternative is to let your home instaed of selling it. In this way, you can generate an income which may give you the freedom to move to another property. However, as with any legal agreement, it is vital that you deal with a reputable company and receive the correct advice.

Progress Properties has many year's experience of letting properties. _Our extensive _____ helps us to find you a reliable and trustworthy tenant._

All our clients have had their finansial records checked. We can gntee that you will not be faced with rental arrears.

Here is some advice which you should follow if you are putting your property up for rental for the fist time.

Your tenants will often want to bring their own furniture.

BILLS AND OUTGOINGS

electrical, gas,

You must ensure that all central heating and hotwater systems are safe, sound and in goood working order. You will be responsible for repairs ~~and maintenance~~ and it is easier if the property is in an excellent state of repair before your tenants move in. _We reccommend that furnishings should be of a reasonable quality._ _Do not over-fill the place with personal items._

APPLIANCES AND FURNISHINGS

It is a sensible precaution to arrange for regular bills
~~You must make arrangements for important outgoings and expenses~~ (such as your mortgage payment, maintenance contracts etc) to be paid by direct debit. This avoids bills arriving at the rental property where they may be ignored. As managing agents, Progress Properties can pay bills on your behalf, but only if there is sufficient money to cover them.

COUNCIL TAX

Council tax is the responsibility of the tenant. When renting out your home, you should advise your local council that you will no longer be living there. You will only pay council tax when the property is empty, perhaps between rental periods. When the property is unoccupied but furnished, the charge is 50% of the normal rate.

DEPPOSITS

When the managing agent arranges the tenancy, a deposit of ___ ___ ___ is payable by the tenant. This money is paid into a holding a/c where it remains until the end of the rental period. If there is no damage ~~to the property~~ and no unpaid bills, the money will be refunded in full.

INSURANCE

(Inset this paragraph 40 mm from left margin)

Your property must be adequately covered for letting purposes. Ensure that you inform your insurance firm as fail%ure to tell them about the lease may invalidate your policy.

(These paragraphs only in single linespacing)

INVENTROY

Before letting to a tenant, it will be necessary to prepare an inventory. This lists every item[1] which you are leaving for the tenant's use. You may prepare it yourself, or you may wish to leave this task to us.

A copy of the inventory is given to the tenant at the beginning of the tenancy. A representative from our firm will normally be present to check it through. If there are any discrepancies, these will be high lighted so that the items can be produced or removed from the list.

A detailed inventory should avoid misunderstandings or disputes. Any losses or breakages will be charged to the tenant.

[1] Furniture, utensils, crockery etc

INSPECTIONS

FRom time to time, we will inspect your property to ensure that it is being well maintained. Under the terms of the agreement, notice must be given. We usually aim to give one week's notice.

RENT

Rent is payable on the first[2] day of each calendar moth. It is exclusive of council tax, water rates, gas, electricity and telephone charges which are the responsibility of the tenant.

Progress Properties sets up a direct debit arrangement with the tenant. ~~We make certain that all payments will be automatically collected on your behalf~~ Any non-payment of fees will be investigated immed

If you require any additional info, please contact a member of our lettings team on 024 7647 0033. They have a wealth of experience and will be delighted to give you advice and guidance.

We await your call!

[2] except 1 January

RESOURCE SHEET

DOCUMENT 1 – Letter

A flat would rent out for approximately £750. A family home would achieve £1,500 per calendar month. Office space is calculated per square metre.

DOCUMENT 2 – Minutes

The person who was successful at interview was Jo Henson.

DOCUMENT 3 – Article

People wanting to find rental accommodation are placed on our database.

An inventory is prepared by the lettings staff.

Deposits amount to 6 weeks' rental charge.

A direct debit arrangement is made with the tenant.

WORD PROCESSING LEVEL 3 PRACTICE EXAMS

WITH HINTS SHEETS COVERING

- Skills Checklist
- General Hints
- Hints for Each Document

HINTS FOR EXAM WORK: OCR WORD PROCESSING LEVEL 3

Checklist of skills

You need to be able to carry out the following before you attempt the practice exams:

- recall the text and amend as instructed
- select and insert paragraphs into a file
- add automatic page numbering
- alter existing and insert new page breaks
- add headers and footers
- adjust line length by altering margins
- inset from both margins, justify and centre text
- alter linespacing, and leave vertical and horizontal space
- emphasise and underline text
- interpret amendment and correction signs
- change specified words automatically by using find and replace facility
- move and copy text by using cut/copy and paste facility
- present information in tables format with vertical headings, ruling and shading
- present information in newspaper columns
- produce a booklet-style document printed in landscape
- insert a text box, and insert and resize a picture
- number items automatically
- produce extra copies and show routing
- sort lists in alphabetical, numerical and chronological order
- alter font type and size
- select and incorporate information from a resource sheet
- use the track changes facility.

General

- Save each document under a separate file name.
- Use either the **Header** or **Footer** facility to record your name, centre number and document number (together with automatic page numbering on a multi-paged document) on each printout.
- Recall text for these exams is available on the Hodder Plus website at **www.hodderplus.co.uk/ocrtextprocessing**.
- Thereafter click on the **Save** icon frequently as you edit the document.
- As a general rule, in these exam units, key in the extra text first and then carry out editing instructions. Leave any linespacing and vertical space editing to the end.
- As you key in an email or internet address, your computer changes the text colour to blue and underscores it. It can be left like this.
- You may print as often as you wish, both during and immediately after the exam time allocation. However, remember that the process is time-consuming, particularly when many candidates are involved, so you should proofread carefully from the screen prior to printing.
- Proofread a second time from the hard copy.
- **Ensure you have SAVED your final edited version of each document before you log off at the end of the session.**

Document 1: report/article

- Recall the stored document as instructed.
- Key in handwritten text first then carry out editing instructions, ticking them off as you complete them.
- To adjust line length by changing margins use **File ➤ Page Setup** (you need to be in *Print Layout View*). Click the justify icon. *NB: A4 paper is 21 cm wide.*
- To set up headers and footers use **View ➤ Header and Footer ➤** select the **Switch Between Header and Footer** icon. Key in the data using the font style and size specified, and in the position required. Use the scroll bars and icons or up and down cursor arrows as you would in the body of the text.
- To start numbering from a specific number use **Insert ➤ Page Numbers**. This allows you to fully customise your numbering, place and position.
- To **Move** or **Copy** text, carry out the following:
- when you **Move** a section of text it should appear *once* in the document – use the **Cut** and **Paste** icons.
- when you **Copy** a section of text it should appear *twice* in the document – use the **Copy** and **Paste** icons. In these exercises you need to copy the text twice, so it will appear three times in your document.
- When transposing items vertically, remember to switch the position of the circled words only and be careful not to omit any intervening text.

- To sort a list use **Table** ➤ **Sort** ➤ **Ascending**.
- To insert a text box use **Insert** ➤ **Textbox**, dragging it to the required size. To make text wrap round all sides of the box right click the box and select **Format Text Box** ➤ select **Layout** ➤ select **Square**.
- To change recurring words in the document use **Edit** ➤ **Replace** and enter the word to be found, then the replacement word. Select **Replace All**.
- When insetting text use **Format** ➤ **Paragraph** ➤ **Indents and Spacing** ➤ select **Indentation** and key in exact measurements for **Left** and **Right**.
- Proofread carefully and use the **Spellcheck**, and check that you have not omitted or replaced text.
- To alter the page breaks in the document use the *Show/Hide* icon to reveal the hard page break, highlight and delete it. To insert a new one, put your cursor where the new page should start and press **Control** and **Enter**.
- Leave linespacing and vertical spacing alterations to the end.

Document 2: two column article/information sheet

- It is easier to work with columns in *Print Layout View*, otherwise columns are displayed underneath each other and not side by side.
- Before keying or making any amendments, turn on track changes using **Tools** ➤ **Track Changes** ➤ **Highlight Changes** ➤ make sure *Track changes while editing*, *Highlight changes on screen* and *Highlight changes in printed document* are ticked and click **OK**. You have to print one copy of the finished document showing the track changes and one copy without them. To remove the track changes go back into **Highlight Changes** and cancel the ticks from all three boxes, click **OK**. Note some packages use a different method. Refer to the help pages of your version for more details on how to do this.
- Complete keying in and editing before formatting text into columns. Unequal column lengths are acceptable.
- To format columns, highlight the text then use **Format** ➤ **Columns** ➤ select the number of columns required and key in the width.
- This document will contain an instruction to insert information to be found in the Resource Sheet. Be careful to include the requested information only.
- **Remember to produce two printouts, one with the track changes and one without.**

Document 3: table

- The table is designed to be displayed on a single sheet of A4 portrait paper.
- Use the tables function and work in *Page Layout View*.
- To insert a table use **Table** ➤ **Insert** ➤ **Table** ➤ select **Columns** and 2 **Rows**. Create more rows as required by positioning your cursor in the last column and pressing the tab key.

- The table should be ruled; if the gridlines are not showing use **Format** _ **Borders and Shading** ➤ select **Gridlines**. You can call up the tables toolbar by using **View** ➤ **Toolbars** ➤ **Tables and Borders**.
- Key each line horizontally, using the tab key or cursor to move between cells.
- Some headings will be vertical. Key in the heading, highlight it then use **Format** ➤ **Text Direction** ➤ click on the vertical box under **Orientation**.
- Follow draft for capitalisation.
- To set a decimal tab, position your cursor in the place where you need the decimal tab, or select the whole column and click the tab selector on the far left of the top ruler line until ⊥ appears (shows decimal tab). Click on the ruler line at the point in the table where the decimal tab is required. Use the tab key to reach the decimal tab column and key in the figures, which should automatically align at the decimal point.
- **Save** your work as soon as you have keyed in all the text. If some of your work is lost when editing the table, you should be able to recall the document at the point that you last saved it.
- Remember to insert the information from the Resource Sheet, as instructed, keying it in the correct column order.
- Column widths can easily be altered by dragging the borders with the mouse.
- To sort text, highlight the sections of the table that need rearranging and use **Table** ➤ **Sort** ➤ **Ascending**.
- Extra line spaces can be inserted by pressing **Enter** from within the cell
- Use **Table** ➤ **Merge Cells** to allow headings to cover more than one column.
- To change the order of columns/sections use **Table** ➤ **Select Column** or **Select Row**, using the **Cut** and **Paste** icons to place the text in its new position. Make sure you have left the correct amount of space in which to paste the selected text.
- Proofread carefully, checking that headings and columns are aligned consistently and that the correct details have been added.
- You will be instructed to modify the table by shading a section, removing lines or changing the style of lines. Print one copy of the table without these modifications and one showing the changes. Make sure the text is legible when printed.

Document 4: booklet/programme/leaflet

- This document is designed to be printed on two sides of landscape A4 paper, so that it can be folded to make a four-page booklet/leaflet.
- To work in landscape use **File** ➤ **Page Setup** ➤ **Paper Size** ➤ choose **Landscape** and make sure you are in *Print Layout View.*

- You can use **File** ➤ **Page Setup** and on the Margins tab, in the Multiple pages section, select **2 pages per sheet** or **book fold** to create your booklet. Alternatively, you can use the columns facility, using **Format** ➤ **Columns** ➤ select **Two** ➤ make sure *Equal columns* is ticked. Note that some software versions may have different options; consult the help pages of your software for further information on how to do this.
- Change the recall text so it matches the font specified for your main document. You will also be instructed to change the style or size of another section of text.
- Follow the order of the draft so that you complete the inside before starting a second page for the outside.
- To copy and insert paragraphs from a stored document use the *Copy* and *Paste* icons.
- To insert a stored picture, choose the correct one, using the filename given, and insert it into the position shown on the draft. To adjust the size, right click the picture ➤ **Format Picture** ➤ **Size** ➤ **Adjust Height/Width**.
- Use the *Centre* icon or **Ctrl + E** to centre the section of text over the typing line on the pages as indicated in the draft. Remember to return to left align at the end of that section.
- Use the *Underline* icon to underline the section of text indicated in the draft. Make sure that it does not extend to the spaces either side of the first and last word in the section.
- The best results are achieved by printing on both sides of one sheet of landscape paper, making sure they match, so that the document can be folded to make a four-page leaflet. However, you will not be penalised for printing out on 2 sides of A4 as long as the orientation and position of pages are correct.
- Proofread carefully, checking that the pages are in the correct order.

EXAM WP 3.A1

Recall the article stored as BATHROOMS and amend as shown. Adjust left and right margins to produce a line length of 10.5 cm. Change to double linespacing (except where indicated) and use full justification. Delete existing page breaks and insert new page breaks as appropriate. Number the pages starting with page 21. Print one copy.

(✓) BATHS ~~AND~~ ~~OR~~ SHOWERS

Change all occurrences of MECHANISMS to SYSTEMS throughout this document matching case as draft

(A)

You will find an extensive range of ~~high quality~~ low/level and standard height shower trays, ingenious bath screens, water delivery mechanisms and copious accessories from which to select.

to give you a truly versatile bathing experience

Copy to points marked ©

For more detailed information and the opportunity to view some of our wonderful displays, register your interest by sending an email to the address at the end of the article.

(B)

This section only in single linespacing

Outward Opening Doors
Bath Screens
Bath Panels
Inward Opening Doors
Shower Unit Mechanisms
Sliding Doors
Optic Light Trays
Trays
Accessories

Sort into exact alphabetical order

INWARD, OUTWARD OR SLIDING DOORS

Sliding door enclosures have 6 mm thick glass bonded directly onto the tray and come with a choice of frame colours. Outward opening doors are designed with hinges or pivots. Inward opening doors provide the smallest bathroom with more space.

BATH SCREENS AND PANELS

can accommodate

Not everybody ~~has the space for both~~ a shower enclosure and a bath. Designs range from a superb minimalist look to a practical yet attractive look. Curved bath screens offer compatibility with many corner baths.

Inset this paragraph 1.5 cm from both left and right margins

Bath panels come in a variety of colours and finishes and can enhance the overall appearance of your new bathroom.

(C)

More to point marked ©

Half the fun of renewing your bathroom is in the research and decision making. Some of the choices you will have to make are

Move to point marked Ⓐ

Once you have taken the decision and set your price limit, relax and enjoy designing this very important room in your house.

SHOWER UNIT MECHANISMS

Power showers also use hot and cold water. They mix the water as required and an integral pump boosts the flow ~~of water~~ to provide a more forceful spray. You should not use a power shower with high pressure water mechanisms.

are economic as they

Electric showers only take water from the mains cold water supply — where there is a limited supply of hot water (it is ideal). Mixer showers use hot and cold water and blend the supplies to the desired temperature. The flow rate can be improved by fixing a separate pump.

One of the most important decisions to make is the type of shower. There are so many brands on the market you may be for given for feeling confused.

Digital showers take water from the hot and cold water supplies and blend the water to the required temperature.

use a digital processor to

SHOWER TRAYS

Change this sentence to sentence case

THESE ARE MADE TO SURVIVE THE RIGOUR OF EVERYDAY USE. Improvements over recent years mean they are made from a toughened material with a durable acrylic surface. Choose from the more traditional standard height shower trays which you step up and into or simulate the wetroom look with a solid surface tray. If you want to make an ultra modern statement, why not introduce optic lighting for a stunning effect.

Insert a text box with border 4.5 cm wide × 4 cm high with the words OPTIC LIGHTING Ensure text box is centred horizontally within the paragraph and that text wraps around the text box on all sides.

Ⓒ

Insert HOME IMPROVEMENTS as a header at the left margin and BATHROOMS as a footer at the right margin. Use Times New Roman 10 font for header and footer. Header and footer to appear on every page

EXAM WP 3.A2

Recall the information sheet stored as TILES and amend as shown ensuring that track changes are displayed. Display the whole document in 2 columns (newspaper style) each column 6 cm wide. Do not change font style or size and retain full justification.

(TILING YOUR BATHROOM WALLS)

(FREE INFORMATION SHEET)

grout and adhesive spreaders,

Ensure that you have the ~~right tools~~ ~~correct implements~~. You will need a tile cutter, spirit level, tile cutting jig and tile spacers.

Mark the bottom of the lowest row of tiles. Your spirit level will help to keep everything straight. It is a good idea to lay out your tiles starting from the centre before you start to fix them to the wall. Adjust to ensure best fit.

(Prior to starting, your bathroom must be clean and dry.)

When you are tiling a bathroom, check that you are using a waterproof tiling adhesive or your tiles may fall off when they are wet.

Adhesive is ~~normally~~ sold ready mixed although you can buy adhesives which require you to add water. [Apply some adhesive and use the edge of the spreader to make horizontal ridges. Place a tile in the position you marked out previously and put a tile spacer between the tiles to keep the spacing even. You can use a damp sponge to wipe away any excess adhesive.

You will undoubtedly have
~~It might be necessary at some point~~ to cut tiles. It is sensible to do this when you have completed the main area. Score across the face of the tile and use the tile cutter to complete the task.

Refer to Resource Sheet and insert the paragraph on grouting and sealing the tiles here

Continue to tile to the end of the row.

Print one copy displaying the track changes. Accept all changes and print a second copy which does not show the track changes.

RESOURCE SHEET – DOCUMENT 2

Deciding on the right tiles for your bathroom can be a daunting task, but most suppliers will offer you samples to take home so that you can see how they look in your bathroom. Once you have chosen your tiles, you need to spend time preparing the area to be tiled.

Grouting and sealing the tiles is the final task, but allow time for the adhesive to dry. Only waterproof grout should be used. Use the spreader and ensure all gaps are filled. Use the damp sponge to clean excess grout.

EXAM WP 3.A3

Key in the following table using Arial 10 font. Rule as shown. Refer to the Resource Sheet for completion of the table. Print one copy in portrait. Modify the table as instructed on the Resource Sheet. Print a second copy.

BATHROOM ACCESSORIES

DESCRIPTION OF ITEM	CATALOGUE NUMBER	QUANTITY IN STOCK	FINISHES AS DESCRIBED	
			NORMAL RETAIL PRICE £	SALE PRICE £
Space Saving Furniture				
Floor pedestal washbasin unit in oak, ready assembled	3990	5	230.00	180.00
Vanity chest drawer unit in walnut with 3 soft close drawers	3887	2	509.75	452.75
Wall storage mirrored medicine cabinet with lock	3994	3	254.80	230.00
Miscellaneous Items				
Luxury chrome soap dispenser and holder	5213	10	45.00	35.00
Double robe hook (door fixture) in brushed steel	5643	5	13.50	9.50
Tumbler and holder for 4 toothbrushes	5565	7	22.75	17.50
Towel Warmers and Radiators				

Refer to Resource Sheet and incorporate the data for Towel Warmers and Radiators only to complete the table

Sort CATALOGUE NUMBER column into exact numerical order within each section starting with the lowest. Ensure all corresponding details are also rearranged.

Modify layout so that CATALOGUE NUMBER becomes the first column.

Modify layout so that Miscellaneous Items comes after Towel Warmers and Radiators

RESOURCE SHEET – DOCUMENT 3

DESCRIPTION OF ITEM	CATALOGUE NUMBER	QUANTITY IN STOCK	FINISHES AS DESCRIBED	
			NORMAL RETAIL PRICE £	SALE PRICE £
Towel Warmers and Radiators				
Curved central heating towel warmer in brushed chrome	4213	3	95.00	82.50
Designer radiator in stainless steel with offset panels	4743	1	325.00	299.00
Floor to ceiling towel warmer finished in graphite black	4641	2	315.50	289.50
Shower Units				
Sprayaway white or chrome remote controlled electric shower	6258	8	335.85	299.99
Powerwash exposed valve mixer shower in chrome	6360	4	474.00	450.00
Ceiling fed thermostatic shower valve with adjustable riser	6372	2	228.87	220.00

TABLE MODIFICATION

Please remove the QUANTITY IN STOCK column and add shading to the SALE PRICE
£ column. Print a second copy showing these modifications.

EXAM WP 3.A4

Create this programme using Courier New 12 font. This is the inside of the programme. See overleaf for the outside.

Insert the picture stored as ENSUITE here. Adjust the size to 6 cm wide.

Copy the final paragraph of the document stored as ADVICE and insert here

Print this document on one or two sheets of plain A4 landscape. Ensure that the font style and size are consistent throughout except where indicated otherwise.

JANUARY – TIPS ON TILING

Come and meet Tom. He is an expert on tiling and will introduce you to his handy hints on how to tile walls and floors.

FEBRUARY – UNDERFLOOR HEATING

Be shown how to determine unheated areas in your room. Work out the quantity of materials required and consider the best type of floor covering.

MARCH – GENERAL ADVICE SESSION

Questions will be taken on any home improvement topic.

If the advice sessions prove to be popular, we will introduce further sessions.

We aim to be the best for high quality products and service.

PROGRESS HOME STORE ← (centre this heading)

PROGRAMME

You are invited to a series of advice sessions to be held on the first Saturday of each month at 10 am in our Coventry store.

These sessions will give you the opportunity to speak to the experts and ask those questions you need answered before you decide to undertake that home improvement task yourself. It may confirm that you should think about employing a professional tradesman.

There will be demonstrations, clinics and advice sessions on a variety of topics. If you have any topics for future sessions, please logon to our website and follow the link to submit your ideas.

(This is the front cover)

Progress Group
Progress House
Westwood Way
COVENTRY
CV4 8JQ

Telephone 024 7647 0033
www.progresshomestore.co.uk

(Emphasise this section by changing the font style and size only)

(This is the back cover)

EXAM WP 3.B1

Recall the report stored as SALES and amend as shown. Adjust left and right margins to produce a line length of 13cm. Change to double linespacing (except where indicated) and use full justification. Delete existing page breaks and insert new page breaks as appropriate. Number the pages starting with 12. Print one copy.

CATALOGUE SALES

Listed below are the sections that had clearance sales at the end of the Period.

In line with global trends the ~~overall~~ profits this year were ~~less~~ lower than budgeted. ✓

This report covers the period from April to June 2009.

Home office supplies and equipment
Air conditioning and heating
Electrical kitchen appliances
Games and toys
Health and beauty
Luggage and shopping bags
Garden furniture and tools
Sports and leisure
Watches and jewellery
Bedroom furniture

Sort into exact alphabetical order

Change all occurrences of period to quarter throughout this document matching case as draft

B
COMPUTER EQUIPMENT

Copy to points marked C

This new section will be added to our catalogue with effect from the beginning of next year.

Change this paragraph to upper case

This section will include laptops that have powerful multimedia capabilities. The range will include netbooks for mobility and widescreen laptops for watching films.

CONSERVATORY FURNITURE
C

Inset this paragraph 3 cm from both left and right margins

items made by hand
A local business will supply ~~hand-crafted wicker and rattan furniture~~ suitable for use in conservatories. These items can also be used in garden rooms and summer houses.

Insert CATALOGUE as a header at the centre and DRAFT as a footer at left margin. Use Tahoma font point size 10 for the header and footer. Header and footer to appear on every page.

INCENTIVES

We operated special offers twice per week during this PERIOD in order to keep records current. The most successful was giving customers a discount voucher if they introduced a new customer to us. As soon as the new customer made a purchase then the original customer was given a £20 voucher.

This did cause ~~some~~ administrative problems for our clerical staff and we had to employ one more person.

Ⓐ

INTERNET SALES

this paragraph only in single linespacing

There was a slight increase in internet sales during this time. More people are visiting our web site than in the past and the average amount of time spent perusing on-line items is 30 minutes. Approximately 50 per cent of the people who visit the web site place an order.

STORE CARDS

In May we launched two of our own store cards. These can be used by customers who visit the shop. Next month customers who order via the telephone will be able to use the new store card.

Move to point marked Ⓑ

The other sections did not need to have clearance sales. Due to prevailing economic trends they had not purchased as much stock.

The store card functions as a credit card. It can only be used to buy goods from us and it will not be accepted by other retailers. People can spread the cost of purchases over several months or they can pay the total balance each month. Compound interest is charged on all outstanding balances each month.

TELEPHONE ORDERS

Insert a text box with border 2cm wide x 2cm high with the word SALES. Ensure text box is centred horizontally within the paragraph and that text wraps around the text box on all sides

The number of people placing telephone orders decreased. There was a trend in April towards collecting smaller items from the warehouse shop to avoid paying the delivery charges. However we delivered the majority of large appliances to householders. *Move to point marked Ⓐ*

Factoring in the additional salary required during this incentive made the company a clear profit of just over £5,000 after tax.

TEXTILES

Ⓒ

We have sourced some fine Egyptian cotton which has a minimum of 300 thread count.

EXAM WP 3.B2

Recall the information sheet stored as ENTRY and amend as shown ensuring that track changes are displayed. Display the whole document in 2 columns (newspaper style) each column 6.5 cm wide. Do not change font style or size and retain full justification.

DOOR ENTRY

let all of our employees know

This information sheet is designed to ~~keep members of staff informed regarding~~ the details of the security procedures for the new office building.

All employees must have photographs taken. These will be placed onto ~~plastic~~ door entry cards which will be issued at the end of next week. The photographer will be here on Monday and Tuesday.

employees to spend time with

The receptionist will arrange a staff rota for the photographer who will be in the meeting room on the second floor. // The door entry cards will be required to access each floor from the stairs or lifts. In addition staff will not be able to enter any of the rooms off the main corridor.

Refer to the Resource Sheet and insert the paragraph on the new office being accessible twenty-four hours a day here

All cards have a unique number and a computer makes a record each time someone enters or exits the building. Using these computer records we can determine which members of staff are late for work. Managers will review records on a regular basis.

without using their door cards

is one of the best available but

Take care of your card and any person losing or finding a card should report to the receptionist immediately.

very costly

This system has been ~~extremely expensive~~ for the company to put in place.

Please ask your manager if you have any questions about the above procedures.

Any employee who mislays a card will have to pay for its replacement. The cost will be automatically deducted from monthly salary payments.

Print one copy displaying the track changes. Accept all changes and print a second copy which does not show the track changes.

RESOURCE SHEET

The side door to the building can only be opened with keys. These keys will be kept in the safe next to the reception desk on the ground floor. The rear door will be unlocked during normal working hours.

The new office will be accessible twenty-four hours a day. Outside normal working hours a door card will be needed to gain entry to the building via the main entrance.

The fire doors will be closed at all times, but will not be locked. The fire doors must only be used in an emergency. The doors are alarmed and this alarm will automatically trigger a response from the local fire station.

EXAM WP 3.B3

Key in the following table using Courier New font point size 11. Rule as shown. Refer to the Resource Sheet for completion of the table. Print one copy in portrait. Modify the table as instructed on the Resource Sheet. Print a second copy.

Modify layout so that <u>Central Asia and the Middle East</u> comes after <u>Central America and the Caribbean</u>

PROGRESS GROUP SALES FIGURES

The table below shows the sales figures for all the companies in the group.

TARGET £ (MILLIONS)	ACTUAL £ (MILLIONS)	COMPANY AND AREA	INDUSTRY AND PRODUCTS	
			TYPE OF BUSINESS	PRINCIPAL ITEMS
		Central Asia and the Middle East		
7	8.1	Asian Holdings Audey, Kazakhstan	Textiles	Clothing
4	3.2	Eastern Group Ankara, Turkey	Pottery	Tableware and ornaments
8	7.8	Camel Enterprises Cairo, Egypt	Furniture	Tables and chairs
		<u>England and Wales</u>		

Refer to the Resource Sheet and incorporate the data for <u>England and Wales</u> only to complete the table

		Central America and the Caribbean		
2	2.7	US Associates Kingston, Jamaica	Food	Herbs and spices
1	2.5	Palma Fisheries La Palma, Panama	Fishing	Frozen and dried fish
3	3.4	Highgate Farm Freeport, Grand Bahama	Sugar	Raw sugar cane

Sort the TARGET £ (MILLIONS) column into exact ascending numerical order within each section. Ensure all corresponding details are also rearranged.

Modify layout so that COMPANY AND AREA becomes the first column.

RESOURCE SHEET

TARGET £ (MILLIONS)	ACTUAL £ (MILLIONS)	COMPANY AND AREA	INDUSTRY AND PRODUCTS	
			TYPE OF BUSINESS	PRINCIPAL ITEMS
		England and Wales		
12	11.4	Office Stationers Taunton, Somerset	Stationery	Office supplies
14	12.3	Welsh Technology Tenby, Pembrokeshire	Computing	Laptops
13	12.9	Harding Limited Exeter, Devon	DIY	Decorating materials
		Australiasia		
6	6.2	Rose Blossom Melbourne, Australia	Accessories	Scarves and handbags
8	5.7	The Leather Shop Sydney, Australia	Footwear	Shoes and boots
9	9.6	Kiwi Limited Auckland, New Zealand	Linens	Curtains and bedclothes

TABLE MODIFICATION

Please add shading to the ACTUAL £ (MILLIONS) column and remove the horizontal lines before and after the section Central America and the Caribbean. Print a second copy showing these modifications.

EXAM WP 3.B4

Create this leaflet using Comic Sans MS font, point size 14. This is the inside of the leaflet. See overleaf for the outside.

Copy the third paragraph of the document stored as PRODUCE and insert here

The restaurant was established more than thirty years ago, and since then we have been serving customers the very best in healthy food.

As well as the restaurant where our guests can enjoy meals in pleasant surroundings, we have a produce shop. After dining with us customers often visit the shop to purchase items to take home with them.

The chefs at the Apple Tree are very experienced and make a variety of dishes both for diners and for visitors to the shop.

We have soya products available and these are very popular with customers who are unable to eat dairy products. There is a selection of milk and yoghurts.

We sell an extensive range of nuts and seeds. The best selling varieties are pistachio nuts and hulled sunflower seeds.

Anyone who dines in the restaurant in the early evening will receive a small discount on their food bill.

Print this document on one or two sheets of plain A4 paper landscape. Ensure that the font style and size are consistent throughout except where indicated otherwise

(this is the front cover)

PROGRESS HEALTH FOOD RESTAURANT

The Apple Tree
Horseshoe Parade
CALNE
Wiltshire
SN11 8HM

Telephone 01249 818903

Open for lunch and dinner every day

Set price lunch menu
Children's menu
Buffet lunches on Sundays
Evening delivery service available

(centre this section)

(this is the back cover)

PROGRESS RESTAURANT CHAIN

Insert the picture stored as RESTAURANT here. Adjust the size to 7 cm high

We have plenty of car parking spaces at the rear of the restaurant and there is a bus stop outside the front door.

Established in 1978

(change font style and size for this sentence only)

EXAM WP 3.C1

Recall the article stored as BANKING and amend as shown. Adjust left and right margins to produce a line length of 10.5 cm. Change to double linespacing (except where indicated) and use full justification. Delete existing page breaks and insert new page breaks as appropriate. Number the pages starting with page 23. Print one copy.

Change all occurrences of safety to security throughout this document matching case as draft

to ensure absolute protection of data and to combat fraud

PROGRESS BANKING

over the last few years

There has been a change in banking habits/with a movement towards online banking.

Copy to points marked (P)

Online banking provides a facility for customers to conduct financial transactions on a secure website operated by their financial provider.

Move to point marked (Z)

Many people are apprehensive when they use internet banking for the first time. Our step by step instructions for first time users are regarded as the benchmark in our industry.

~~opportunity~~

An obvious benefit is the ~~facility~~ to do banking at any time of the day or night. This avoids having to fit in with traditional banking hours. Accounts can be accessed at any time. Bills can be paid and money can be transferred.

SAFETY

Safety is a high priority. Progress Banking is committed to providing the highest level of safety for online customers. Account details can be accessed at any time in complete confidence. [We have a stringent programme of safety initiatives which are reviewed constantly.] Our website www.progressbank.co.uk gives ~~full~~ information on our safety measures.

Any money taken from an account through fraudulent activities will be refunded in full provided that the customer has taken reasonable steps to protect confidential data and has fully complied with our terms and conditions.

Insert a text box with border 4cm wide x 2.5cm high with the words DATA PROTECTION Ensure text box is centred horizontally within the paragraph and that text wraps around the text box on all sides

Insert MODERN BANKING as a header at the left margin and INTERNET SERVICES as a footer at the centre. Use Arial 9 font for the header and footer. Header and footer to appear on every page.

CRIMINAL ACTIVITY

Inset this paragraph 2.5 cm from both left and right margins

We ~~work tirelessly to combat the threat from~~ *liaise with other financial providers concerned about* online fraud. We offer the following advice to help provide protection against online crime. ◄

Change this sentence to uppercase

to safeguard against virus damage

All computers should have reliable anti-virus software installed/ Our advice is to avoid opening any email that looks doubtful. Spam emails must be blocked. Computers should be backed up regularly. A modern web browser will identify suspicious websites. Identity theft has become a huge problem and ~~so~~ it is unwise to give too much personal information on social networking sites.

SERVICES

In addition to round-the-clock banking facilities, our help line on 0800 470033 is available to answer customers' queries. *Our staff are fully trained in every aspect of the banking system. Lines are open from 6 am until 10 pm each day.*

Ⓟ

HELP DESK

Ⓩ

Internet banking is very straightforward. Once an account is accessed a customer can

This section only in single linespacing

pay bills
arrange standing orders
confirm account balance
check statements
manage finances
request product information
register for new services
view transactions

Sort into exact alphabetical order

FOREIGN CURRENCY

Customers can order currency for visits to foreign countries. Orders will be delivered within 24 hours provided that they are received before 3.30 pm and that the next day is a working day.

The order [at any time on the website] can be tracked/. *We do not charge commission for travel money orders.*

Move to point marked

Internet banking can offer many advantages over traditional banking in branches, most notably the flexibility and convenience to suit today's busy lifestyle.

Ⓟ

EXAM WP 3.C2

Recall the article stored as ENQUIRY and amend as shown ensuring that track changes are displayed. Display the whole document in 2 columns (newspaper style) each column 6 cm wide. Do not change font style or size and retain full justification.

INSURANCE PROTECTION

TAX ENQUIRY

~~costs incurred~~ ✓

Small companies can take out insurance protection against any ~~financial liabilities~~ should they be the subject of a tax enquiry. These costs can be considerable.

An exhaustive search of a company's financial records will be made. It may cause disruption to the smooth running of the firm and can put an extra burden on personnel. Any company may be selected. Anomalies may have appeared in the annual accounts or it may be a completely random selection.

The organisation will be asked detailed questions. Research into the answers can often take a great amount of time and the information provided must be completely accurate.

incur extra expenditure which could run

Without insurance, the company will ~~be liable for a bill running~~ into thousands of pounds even if, at the end of the enquiry, no irregularities are found. The investigation costs will not be covered by accountants' annual charges. Their fees will be charged at their normal hourly rate.

Refer to the Resource Sheet and insert the paragraph on tax enquiry here

This protection can alleviate any worries associated with the financial costs involved. Your accountant can explain how the cost will be calculated for your company. Ask for information on what is covered by the insurance and, more importantly, what is excluded.

many companies consider it is

The cost of the insurance can be modest and/~~well~~ worth paying in order to have peace of mind.

as they answer detailed questions on your behalf

The ongoing investigation may last for several months.

Print one copy displaying the track changes. Accept all changes and print a second copy which does not show the track changes.

RESOURCE SHEET

Accountancy practices have insurance and can claim the cost of professional fees when acting for clients in a tax enquiry. Your accountant may provide a scheme offering your company protection against the extra expenditure.

Some costs will not be covered. Other restrictions may apply as specified in our covering letter.

If you need further information or need to speak to someone in our practice, please telephone 024 7647 0033 without delay.

EXAM WP 3.C3

Key in the following table using Arial 11 font. Rule as shown. Refer to the Resource Sheet for completion of the table. Print one copy in portrait. Modify the table as instructed on the Resource Sheet. Print a second copy.

Sort SELLING PRICE £ column into exact numerical order within each section starting with the highest. Ensure all corresponding details are also rearranged.

INFORMATION FROM HALF-YEARLY STOCKTAKE

DESCRIPTION OF PRODUCT	REMAINDERS	DETAILED STOCK INFORMATION		REFERENCE CODE
		SELLING PRICE £	STOCK VALUE £	
Refer to Resource Sheet and incorporate the data for ELECTRICAL section only to complete the table				
EQUIPMENT				
Grass trimmer with 23 cm cutting diameter, rotating head and telescopic handle height adjustment	20	24.95	499.00	GT397
Electric rotary mower with integrated rear roller	37	119.99	4439.63	ERM36
Lightweight hedge trimmer with protective blade cover	105	29.99	3148.95	HT24
GARDEN FURNITURE				
Gazebo made from 260 gsm material with water-resistant coating	7	89.99	629.93	GZB45
Patio heater with adjustable heat control and extra wide canopy	14	79.99	1119.86	PH263
Square wooden table set with four upright chairs	4	239.95	959.80	TS968

Modify layout so that REFERENCE CODE becomes the second column

Modify layout so that GARDEN FURNITURE section comes before EQUIPMENT section

RESOURCE SHEET

DESCRIPTION OF PRODUCT	REMAINDERS	DETAILED STOCK INFORMATION		REFERENCE CODE
		SELLING PRICE £	STOCK VALUE £	
ELECTRICAL				
Mains or battery portable multi-format playback DVD	20	49.99	999.80	DVD201
Interactive digibox with electronic programme guide and twin scart sockets	149	15.99	2382.51	DGB49
Home cinema with wireless audio receivers and four satellite speakers	16	169.99	2719.84	HCR94
MISCELLANEOUS				
Large digital safe with electronic lock and 3-8 digit combination code	20	54.99	1099.80	DS380
4-drawer filing cabinet with anti-tilt function and 7-year warranty	16	139.99	2239.84	FC47
Inkjet printer, copier and scanner with auto document feed	12	199.99	2399.88	PCS14

TABLE MODIFICATION

Please add shading to the EQUIPMENT section and corresponding details and change the outside border of the table to dashed line style as shown round this instruction. Print a second copy showing these modifications.

EXAM WP 3.C4

Create this booklet using Comic Sans MS 13 font. This is the inside of the booklet. See overleaf for the outside.

Rules of the Auction ← Centre this line

Payment for all lots is required on the night by cash or cheque. Commission bids must be settled within four days of the auction.

The successful purchaser should contact the donor to finalise arrangements for collection of the promise.

An undisclosed reserve price may be imposed. The organisers will sell to the highest bidder above the reserve.

The description of each lot is based on information supplied by the donor.

No liability is accepted for mistakes, omissions or faults in the auction catalogue.

The auctioneer's decision is final!

Some of the items already on offer are listed below.

A day's coarse fishing

Camping for two nights at Perivale Camping Site

Consultation with chiropractor

Back massage with qualified physiotherapist

An introduction to scuba diving

Vehicle valeting and full MOT

Laser printer and accessories

17" flat screen computer monitor

We are grateful for these generous offers.

Print this document on one or two sheets of plain A4 landscape. Ensure that the font style and size are consistent throughout except where indicated otherwise.

AN AUCTION OF PROMISES

An Auction of Promises is when businesses undertake to donate a service, a skill or an item. Bidders then bid for the lots that interest them. The highest bidder is successful.

Copy the second paragraph of the document stored as AUCTION and insert here

This is the front cover

This is the back cover

Emphasise this sentence by changing the font style and size only

This booklet is sponsored by Progress Play Equipment.

Insert the picture stored as PLAYAREA here. Adjust the size to 8 cm wide

We value our reputation and our business has grown through <u>personal recommendation</u>. Our designs are easy to assemble. We guarantee prompt delivery.

AUDIO-TRANSCRIPTION LEVEL 3 PRACTICE EXAMS

WITH HINTS SHEETS COVERING

- Skills Checklist
- General Hints
- Hints for Each Document

HINTS FOR EXAM WORK: OCR AUDIO-TRANSCRIPTION LEVEL 3

Checklist of skills

You need to be able to carry out the following before you attempt the practice exams:

- use the audio equipment provided by your centre
- recall and use a letterhead
- lay out a letter
- lay out minutes, an advertisement and an itinerary
- alter linespacing
- allocate vertical space
- emphasise and underline text and headings
- correct text as instructed
- insert apostrophes
- create new paragraphs
- present information in tables format
- use decimal tabs
- format numbered paragraphs
- incorporate information announced during the exam
- indicate enclosure(s)
- indicate routing of extra copies
- add automatic page numbering.

General

- Either recall the letterhead template for the first document or start a **New** file.
- You may use either the **Header** or **Footer** facility to record your name, centre number and document number (together with automatic page numbering on any multi-paged document) on each printout.
- Recall a letterhead template into your own new file then use **Save As** to give

it a filename. The template is available on the Hodder Plus website at **www.hodderplus.co.uk/ocrtextprocessing**.

- The dictated documents are all available on the Hodder Plus website.
- Click on the **Save** screen icon frequently as you work.
- Carry out editing instructions as you key in.
- As you key in an email or internet address, your computer may change the text colour and underscore it. It can be left like this in the exam.
- A Candidate Information Sheet is included with each exam. This lists addresses, references and proper nouns. Take care to copy these correctly as the words may be unfamiliar to you.
- You may print as often as you wish, both during and immediately after the exam time allocation.
- Once you have completed a document, replay the tape, listening carefully and checking that the hard copy is correct.
- **Ensure you have SAVED your final edited version of each document before you log off at the end of the session.**

Document 1: letter

- This document must be printed on the OCR letterhead template.
- It must be dated with the date on which are doing the practice exam.
- Key in the *Our ref* as dictated. Do not add your own initials or insert a *Your ref* unless one is given to you.
- The special mark is best placed immediately before the name and address.
- Key in the text, making amendments as dictated.
- Remember that you may need to insert an apostrophe, which is not dictated, in the text to make it grammatically correct.
- Follow capitalisation for the heading and text in the body of the letter as dictated.
- When underlining text, ensure that the line does not overshoot either end of the relevant text. It may include any punctuation that is part of the final word.
- If the document runs to more than a single page, the continuation sheet must be numbered. Use **Insert ➤ Page Numbers** to customise your numbering.
- Indicate any enclosure(s) mentioned in the body of the letter by using Enc/Encs or Att/Atts.
- To route extra copies, key the routing information on the document and print three copies. Tick in pen against the name on one copy and against *File* on the other copy. Routing may also be shown by using a symbol, eg √ or by emboldening, underscoring or highlighting. Pencil marks are not acceptable.
- You may print extra copies and make routing ticks outside the exam time allocation, but you may not key in the copy details at that stage.

- Proofread carefully and use the **Spellcheck**, and check that you have not omitted or misplaced text.

Document 2: minutes/advertisement/itinerary

- You should not date any of these types of document.
- Key in the text, making amendments as dictated.
- Remember that you may need to insert an apostrophe, which is not dictated, in the text to make it grammatically correct.
- Follow capitalisation for the heading, subheadings and text in the body of the document as dictated.
- When emphasising a sentence or paragraph you may embolden, capitalise, underline, alter font style/size, centre or inset. Remember to take the emphasis instruction off at the end of the portion of text.
- When centring an item of text, use the *Centre* icon. Remember to return to left align for the rest of the document.
- Use the ruler line on the left of your screen to check the measurements for your vertical spacing.
- Proofread carefully and use the **Spellcheck**, and check that you have not omitted or misplaced text.

Document 3: report/article

- Key in the text, making the dictated amendments as you go.
- Follow capitalisation for the main heading and text in the body of the letter as dictated. Use your own style for subheadings and table column headings.
- When altering the linespacing of paragraphs of text, ensure that the linespacing between the paragraphs is consistent. Do not forget to change back at the end of the section.
- If the document runs to more than a single page, the continuation sheet must be numbered. Use **Insert** → **Page Numbers** to customise your numbering. Single sheets should not be numbered.
- When numbering paragraphs or items, you can key the numbers as you go, using the tab key to align the following text, or you can use **Format** → **Bullets and Numbering** → select **Numbered**, which will automatically align the text.
- This is the document in which to insert the extra text that is given to you. The dictation will tell you exactly where to insert it.
- This document will include a table. Column widths are dictated for candidates keying the table using the tab key. The following hints apply to those using the tables function.

Displaying tabular work using the tables function

- Work in *Print Layout View*.
- Key each line horizontally, using the tab key or cursors to move between cells.
- Column widths can be altered to your requirements by dragging the column borders with the mouse.
- Extra linespaces can be inserted by pressing **Enter** from within the cell.
- To set a decimal tab, position your cursor in the place where you need the decimal tab, or select the whole column and click the tab selector on the far left of the top ruler line until ⊥ appears (shows decimal tab). Use the tab key to reach the decimal tab column and key in the figures, which should automatically align at the decimal point.
- Gridlines may be used in the table, but a clear linespace should be left below the column headings. Do not leave empty cells.
- To stop the gridlines from printing, use **Format ➤ Borders and Shading ➤ Borders** select **None**.
- Use the **Spellcheck** and proofread carefully, particularly checking you have not omitted or misplaced text.

Accessing audio practice exams material

Candidate Information Sheets and Instructions to Invigilator

Candidate Information Sheets and Instructions to Invigilator (containing extra information to be incorporated) follow for these practice exams:

- AT 3.A – documents 1, 2 and 3
- AT 3.B – documents 1, 2 and 3
- AT 3.C – documents 1, 2 and 3

Templates

The letter templates are available on the Hodder Plus website at **www.hodderplus.co.uk/ocrtextprocessing**. The same templates can be used for each practice exam, but under actual exam conditions you must see the templates provided by OCR for that particular paper.

Dictated documents

The dictation for the above exams is also available on the Hodder Plus website.

EXAM AT 3.A1

CANDIDATE INFORMATION SHEET

Included in dictation:

Angus MacDougall
Hillwalker Insurance Group
Fionn Ramsay
Moon Tang

Address:

Strawberry Cottage
Back Lane
FALKLAND
Scotland
KY15 2FD

Reference(s):

MT/SIC

NB: All other instructions (eg courtesy titles, headings, etc) will be given in the dictation.

EXAM AT 3.A2

CANDIDATE INFORMATION SHEET

Included in dictation:

Marsham Leather Company Ltd
Priti Kumar
Arthur Grant
Canada

Address:

Reference(s):

NB: All other instructions (eg courtesy titles, headings, etc) will be given in the dictation.

EXAM AT 3.A3

CANDIDATE INFORMATION SHEET

Included in dictation:

Labrys School
Business and Enterprise
GCSE
A star
English
French
Mrs Jared

Address:

Reference(s):

NB: All other instructions (eg courtesy titles, headings, etc) will be given in the

INSTRUCTIONS FOR INVIGILATOR

About 15 – 30 minutes after the start of the examination, announce that for Document 3

pupils or friends now have the benefit of a peer mediation group.

EXAM AT 3.B1

CANDIDATE INFORMATION SHEET

Included in dictation:

Megan Summerfield
Jasmine Begum
Highways Department
Mohammed Singh

Reference:

DR/WH

Address:

The Old Stables
26 Holly Drive
ST AUSTELL
Cornwall
PL25 6BG

NB: All other instructions (eg courtesy titles, special mark, extra copies, headings etc) will be given in the dictation

EXAM AT 3.B2

CANDIDATE INFORMATION SHEET

DOCUMENT 2

Included in dictation:

Reference:

Address:

NB: All other instructions (eg courtesy titles, special mark, extra copies, headings etc) will be given in the dictation.

EXAM AT 3.B3

CANDIDATE INFORMATION SHEET

Included in dictation:

Bluebell Wood

Reference:

/

Address:

/

NB: All other instructions (eg courtesy titles, special mark, extra copies, headings
        etc) will be given in the dictation.

INSTRUCTIONS FOR INVIGILATOR

About 15-30 minutes after the start of the examination, announce that for Document 3

This spacious residence is adjacent to the old mill house.

EXAM AT 3.C1

CANDIDATE INFORMATION SHEET

Included in dictation:

Jeremy Allison
Manor Hotel
James Proudfoot
Customer Service Manager
Area Manager

References:

JF/RT

Address:

14 Redman Street
WORCESTER
WR2 3AN

NB: **All other instructions (eg courtesy titles, special mark, extra copies, headings etc) will be given in the dictation.**

EXAM AT 3.C2

CANDIDATE INFORMATION SHEET

Included in dictation:

Coventry
London Euston
Progress International
Westwood Way
Mr Andrew Dawson
The Lobster Pot
Mrs June Merton
Dudley

References:

Address:

NB: All other instructions (eg courtesy titles, special mark, extra copies, headings etc) will be given in the dictation.

EXAM AT 3.C3

CANDIDATE INFORMATION SHEET

Included in dictation:

References:

Address:

NB: All other instructions (eg courtesy titles, special mark, extra copies, headings etc) will be given in the dictation.

INSTRUCTIONS TO INVIGILATOR:

About 15-30 minutes after the start of the examination, announce that for

Document 3:

These fees are usually based on a percentage of annual turnover.